DC

Stop Procrastination

Paul Swanson

CONTENTS

How To Read This Book

I want to offer some tips I've learned about reading books, especially useful ones like this, before we get started.

1. Feel free to read a book in any order or manner you like; there are no rules to reading a book.

2. Skip the sections that don't apply to you. No, you don't need to read a book from beginning to end.

3. To help you recall more, highlight content and make notes.

4. It can be useful to skim a book before reading it. I frequently skim books in order to choose what I should pay attention to or skip. I occasionally learn that I can't skip anything. I occasionally skip chapters in books.

5. You simply need one thought to completely transform your life. A book is already worthwhile of your time if it offers you only one sound piece of advice.

Happy reading.

PART I

Overcoming Procrastination

Do It Today, Not Tomorrow

I had an excuse for every time I put off making a decision, pushed the snooze button, skipped the gym, or didn't do my tasks because I didn't feel like it.

I justified my fatigue to myself. Or perhaps it could wait until the following day. Who gives a damn if you put anything off? You should care, I suppose. mostly because your life is entirely your responsibility. We frequently mistakenly believe that productivity hacks, applications, or technologies will solve all of our issues. But it also implies that we give ourselves permission to attribute our lack of productivity to outside factors.

- "No, it's not me, it's my old laptop. It sucks, and I can't work this way."
- "The office is too loud."
- "People keep calling and emailing me."
- "I never have time."

It takes inner strength to fight procrastination. In my own life, I can think of a lot of instances like that. I thought my career was trapped in 2013. Prior to it, my father and I founded a business two years before. However, after two years, I grew impatient because I yearned to accomplish more and learn more. I thus took on some freelancing. I created websites, worked in design, content marketing, and copywriting. However, it didn't fly off. Why? I never performed the unpleasant tasks. To avoid those challenging chores, I instead obtained a job.

All of us occasionally flee.

Building a company or a career is challenging. You have to perform demanding, tiresome, and unfulfilling activities. Nobody is going to hand you additional clients or employment if you want it. You must work hard. Use any strategy you like to expand your business, whether it's content marketing, networking, or one-on-one sales.

Additionally, you must establish partnerships, be strategic, surpass your goals, and be outstanding at what you do if you want to go up the corporate ladder.

You SHOULD act in that way, right? Most of us are already aware of these facts. Or you'll learn about it. There isn't a trick to getting forward at work. However, we would rather avoid employment. And to me, that is the essence of procrastination. You are aware of what needs to be done, yet you choose not to. Instead, you access a news website and begin reading pointless articles. Or perhaps you dislike your life and go through your Instagram account without like a single photo. You might visit Mr. Porter, Net-A-Porter, Zara, H&M, or any other online retailer you enjoy.

That was the tale of my life, and to some extent, it still is. For instance, I'm now writing a new novel. I am aware of the subject and have a title. However, I find writing to be a really challenging task.

So I search for solace. In order to manage my business, I respond to emails, read articles, go out for coffee, shop online, and complete ongoing projects. Not like I'm unorganised or anything. I'm warring with myself, which is why. In his groundbreaking book The War Of Art, Steven Pressfield refers to this internal foe as Resistance. To which he responds, "Resistance is always false and full of trash."

Do It Today, Not Tomorrow

That is something I have to constantly remind myself of. When you put off doing anything, you constantly want to do it later. I remain that way. We are probably hardwired to do it. I now rely on a system to live a successful, joyful, and meaningful life, which is a minor but significant departure from three years ago.

I didn't know how to do things back then. Always feeling stuck, miserable, and frustrated, I gave up easily. But now I know how to get beyond my difficulties. What I did was as follows:

- I regularly hone my mental fortitude. My brain used to be neglected. I was psychologically unsteady, over-thought, and self-reliant. It wasn't for want of ability on my part. It was because I lacked confidence in my capacity to solve problems. I then began reading about Stoicism, Pragmatism, and Mindfulness—basically anything that could help me better manage my thoughts and build mental toughness. I don't want to be my thoughts' master. I favour the contrary.

- Every day, I work out my body. When I don't work out, I get restless and lack confidence, enthusiasm, and attention. I keep my mind and body in shape so I'm always prepared for battle. I discovered that the battle against procrastination must begin before the battle itself. Surely even soldiers receive training before going to battle? Be in excellent bodily and mental health. Always.

- I follow a set of regular routines that give me control over my life. I keep a notebook, read, establish daily goals, and avoid consuming pointless information. Human interaction is crucial, therefore I make sure to engage with my friends and family every day. This keeps me in my place. I don't have big hopes for the future. And my days are enjoyable. I never look beyond than that.

• I constantly have a list of quick but crucial activities to finish. Take my most recent book, for instance. I frequently want to run away from challenging situations, like actually sitting down and writing. I thus convince myself that this is a bad day. But each time I get that thought, I go to my list of little jobs and start working on one of them TODAY.

• To communicate my ideas, I research and put persuasive science into practise. "You can be the best writer and instructor in the world, but if no one knows about it, you can't have an impact," my mentor once said to me. You may create better pitches, cover letters, website text, emails, etc. by using the principles of persuasion.

Naturally, building the groundwork for this strategy takes time. There is a lot more to it than that. It's not magic, though. However, leading a fruitful life is also not simple. Additionally, technology or hacks are not at all relevant. It involves creating a solid foundation upon which to base your life, career, and business. What is your plan for leading a fruitful life?

Whatever it is: Work on it today. Not tomorrow.

What I Do When I Can't Focus

Do you have trouble completing your tasks? Are notifications, rumours, or other strange things keeping you from your work all the time? Then we are similar, you and I. Because one of the most difficult things to do at work is to focus on a single thing. You know that something always comes along to disturb you?

- Another person
- A call
- A meeting
- A false emergency
- Your cat
- A stranger's cat
- News about last night's NBA game

Yes, you can blame them, but that would be unfair. We both understand that none of those things may interrupt you without your consent. That implies that whenever you are not fully present, you are granting someone or something permission to do so. Unsettling, huh?

That's how I view disruptions, actually. But I have to admit that sometimes it's difficult for me to stay focused. I acquiesce on occasion. This is bad. Gossiping, checking Instagram 439 times per day, watching 49 YouTube videos, and reading unfavourable news doesn't improve your life. What can you do, then, to sharpen your focus? Here are 2 things I always do when I find it difficult to concentrate on the important stuff.

1. Eliminate. Eliminate. Eliminate

We accumulate things daily. I'm not only referring to the items you purchase, such as clothing, kitchenware, home accents, toys, electronics, or anything. We build up thoughts. Have you ever given it any thought? We are exposed to so many ideas that some of them become our own as a result. For instance, a lot of people have encouraged me to make more YouTube videos. Everyone has ideas, including my family, friends, coworkers, readers, and pupils. They also wish to assist.

In a same vein, I likewise impart my views to others. Ideas on how to enhance your relationships, profession, business, or quality of life. We all engage in it. There is nothing improper about that. If you don't filter the input you receive from individuals, it will simply become a problem. I therefore thought to myself, "Hey! I should make YouTube videos after hearing from people that I should." I ought to upload videos to YouTube!

That's something I've been considering a lot for the past six months. I spent a lot of time developing a plan as well. "What should the topic of my videos be? Where should I put them on tape? How ought I to alter them? Which songs should I play? I've put a lot of effort into it. I also recently released a video. Positive feedback was received. Only one issue exists: It takes up too much of my time and attention. I'm able to spend less time writing, podcasting, and developing new courses as a result.

And those are the exact actions I want to take. I began a blog because I enjoy writing and am skilled at it. Because of this, the labour is simpler than making YouTube videos, which I'm not very good at. In addition, I genuinely enjoy creating the content for my online courses, books, and articles. I don't mind when the work becomes challenging. But I found myself getting really agitated as I worked on the YouTube videos. Again, it affected my ability to concentrate and my work. What did I do when I couldn't concentrate? What could I get rid of to simplify my life and make it easier to concentrate? I asked myself.

I stopped concentrating on YouTube in this situation. My main method is elimination, and I apply it to many areas of my life. Over the years, we gather so much extra baggage that we constantly need to get rid of it:

- Ideas
- Projects
- Work
- Objects
- And so forth

Try this approach if you have trouble focusing. Make it easy to live by simplifying your life. And let's be upfront about this. Who wants to lead an impossible life? Life is difficult enough as it is. Don't complicate matters.

2. Think About Past Success

Serotonin, a chemical neurotransmitter our cells make, is stimulated by thoughts of previous success and enjoyment. The primary molecule that has an impact on every system in your body is serotonin. Our bodies' physiological processes depend greatly on serotonin. But it also aids in lowering anxiety, boosting libido, balancing mood, and stabilising mood.

Additionally, serotonin is crucial to our overall health. But here's why serotonin is important for maintaining focus. Delay in gratification is also regulated by serotonin. A decrease in serotonin activity can eventually result in a lack of focus. Less likely are you to carry out your plans. There's a good likelihood that your serotonin activity is low when you lose attention. That is why you indulge in activities that only give you temporary pleasure, such as going out, drinking, shopping, engaging in sexual activity, watching television, or any other such activity.

Increase the activity of your serotonin to sharpen your focus. Exercise can achieve that, according to research. A simple mind-exercise, however, is another option that is both equally effective and far simpler. All you have to do is reflect on past instances of success. The Upward Spiral author Alex Korb, a neuroscientist at UCLA, explains why remembering happy memories helps you concentrate on what matters:

Remembering good things that have happened in your life is all it takes to raise serotonin levels. The anterior cingulate cortex, which is located right behind the prefrontal cortex and regulates attention, produces more serotonin as a result of this straightforward action.

Your focus improves as serotonin levels rise. That's ultimately what you ought to do. Even though it may sound corny, you have to repair problems when they arise.

The first thing I do when I can't concentrate is admit that I have an issue that needs to be solved. Some people live their lives completely unaware that they are struggling.

No, it's not natural to gossip constantly, check your phone every two minutes, or be bored.

Think about your life. Consider what is important to you. Then, carry out those actions without becoming sidetracked; keep on the route. All the best!

How To Beat Procrastination (backed by science)

Since the dawn of human civilisation, there has been procrastination. Procrastination is the adversary of results, according to numerous historical luminaries including Herodotus, Leonardo Da Vinci, Pablo Picasso, Benjamin Franklin, Eleanor Roosevelt, and thousands more. Abraham Lincoln once said: "You cannot avoid the burden of tomorrow by evading it now." This is one of my favourite procrastination quotes.

The ironic thing about procrastination is that we are all aware of its negative effects. Who genuinely enjoys putting things off? Nobody likes to do that. neither do I. However, my life was a storey of procrastination. Every semester when I was a college student, this would occur: At the start of every semester, I was the coolest guy on the earth. I'm unwinding, going out, and having fun. Really big.

I was completely stress-free. But a week before my tests, I would start to panic.

Why didn't you start sooner, dude? I'd tell myself that. And then I'd start freaking out when I was studying, locking myself in my room with a bunch of Red Bull cans. Procrastination may make you feel better in the short term, but it will hurt you in the long run, according to study. It truly doesn't matter why you put off doing something. Some people enjoy the stress of deadlines. Some people wait until the very last minute because they are terrified to fail.

Procrastination has a cost, which is something that all doers of it share. The cost of procrastination is covered in this widely read article by Dianne Tice and Roy Baumeister, which was published in the American Psychological Society magazine. It has to do with:

- Depression
- Irrational beliefs
- Low self-esteem
- Anxiety
- Stress

The practise of procrastination is not innocent. It's an indication of insufficient self-control. Researchers also draw parallels between procrastination and drug and alcohol dependence. It is serious. And I've been dealing with that for a long time. It was difficult for me to begin and finish work in the years after I graduated from college. The tendency of procrastinating just creeps into your life. You can't just easily shake it. It went like this every time I had a business concept or wanted to start something:

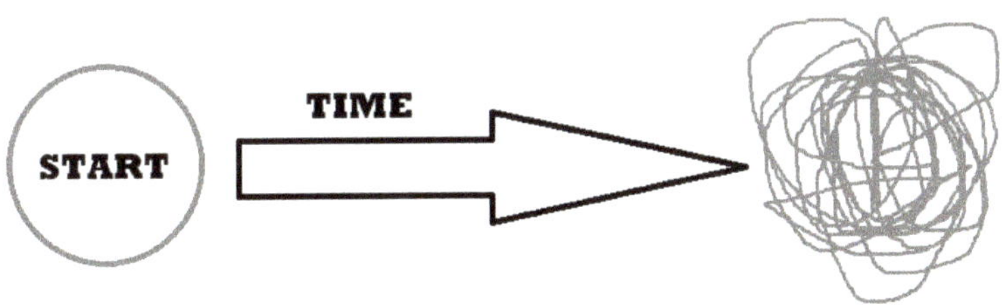

I would start whenever I had an idea or a goal, but along the road, something would go wrong. I went from beginning to complete anarchy. Distractions, competing priorities, missed opportunities, failure, negative self-talk, and other obstacles would stand in the way. And the outcomes are consistent: You never do anything.

Beating Procrastination

The study by Dianne Tice and Roy Baumeister's main finding, in my opinion, is this: "The present evidence implies that procrastinators enjoy themselves rather than working at given activities, until the mounting pressure of impending deadlines pushes them to get to work. According to this theory, procrastination might result from a lack of self-control and a reliance on other stimuli to encourage labour.

We overrate our capacity for self-control, self-regulation, and willpower. We believe, "Sure, I'll write a novel in three weeks." We all think we're brilliant and psychologically tough. But when the task is required, we falter. If you procrastinate, you will inevitably put off doing your work. Both minor and large tasks fall under this, too.

Everyone is afraid to leave their comfort zone, which is why those spaces are called comfort zones. To conduct a risky action requires guts. However, completing simple things like filing your taxes, paying your bills, printing something for your boss, etc. doesn't need much bravery. The truth is that procrastination has nothing to do with your goals; no matter how big or tiny, they can wait. There is always tomorrow, right?

The slope of procrastination is the point between the beginning and the conclusion of a task when you give in to one distraction. And that's precisely the point at which you stop working.

When you first begin a task, you are enthusiastic and concentrated, but after some time you think, "Let's read the news for a minute." There is only ever one thing that comes first. Then you decide: I might as well watch one Game of Thrones episode. Then, another YouTube video followed by a third. After that, I looked through Instagram for a while. ... and so on. "This is the last time I'm wasting my time," is how it always ends. Right, I see.

Willpower Doesn't Work. Systems Do.

You actually need a system for carrying out your work. Many people avoid routines, structures, and frameworks because they prefer "freedom" I'm sorry to break your heart, but freedom is your adversary. The truth is that you need rules in order to accomplish your goals. What are some strategies that research has shown to work?

- Self-imposed deadlines.
- Accountability systems (commitment with friends, or a coach).
- Working/studying in intervals.
- Exercising 30 minutes a day.
- A healthy diet.
- Eliminating distractions.
- And most importantly: Internal motivation.

A productivity system can be created by combining the appropriate productivity techniques. Deadlines engender urgency, accountability fosters responsibility, working in intervals sharpens your attention, physical activity and a balanced diet offer you more energy, and removing distractions removes temptations. However, if you lack an inner drive, no system can assist you. People complicate the question "Why do you do what you do?" much too much.

if you are unaware. Create something. Even the most tedious jobs become bearable if you have a purpose in mind. It will eventually fit into the overall scheme. Take a step back, consider why you do what you do, and then rely on a system that supports that instead of jumping right into work. Not a difficult concept. only science.

How To Stop Wasting Time and Improve Your Personal Effectiveness

It's easy to understand why I study productivity. According to me, happiness and productivity go hand in hand. Additionally, you will rise in your profession more quickly if you are more productive than the average person. You gain new knowledge. You work harder. and eventually receive greater rewards.

And when I discuss productivity, I also discuss effectiveness. Because productivity does not imply that you do the proper tasks. It just means you accomplish a lot of things. But it is not important.

However, effectiveness relates to doing the proper things. And that's what counts most if you want to do your work well, make money, have a fulfilling life, or gain new abilities. If not, all you do is circle about. Even though you appear busy, nothing worthwhile will be accomplished. In other words, it's simple to complete pointless tasks. Work that doesn't advance your pursuit of your goals.

Results matter the most.

In real terms, that means you can work 50 hours a week, but if you don't advance personally, emotionally, or financially, you won't be productive. Where should I start, they frequently ask me. I'd like to share an activity from my productivity course, Procrastinate Zero, to help you answer that question.

I learned this activity from Peter Drucker's book The Effective Executive. In my opinion, Drucker is the pioneering and preeminent thinker on knowledge worker effectiveness. Drucker, who essentially coined the term "personal effectiveness," has had some influence on many of the books, articles, productivity tools, and productivity apps you find today.

The next section has a straightforward exercise from The Effective Executive that you may use to improve your own effectiveness. I slightly changed it for ease of use.

Step 1: Know Thy Time

I often hear people saying: "I don't know what's wrong with me. I keep procrastinating."

My question is: "Do you know thy time?"

It's difficult to quit procrastinating or increase your productivity if you don't track your time. Because you need to be aware of where your time goes first if you want to manage it better. You can't only rely on your recollection. Would you be able to tell me what you were doing at this precise time one week ago if I asked you? You're all set.

How do you determine the time? Log your activities. I frequently ask customers to keep an activity journal for two weeks prior to our actual appointment. An activity journal is exactly what it sounds like: a detailed account of your daily activities, hour by hour.

It doesn't matter which technique you use for your activity log. It is only important that you keep a record for at least two weeks. You would prefer a full month's worth of activities to be recorded.

I simply have a pen and a notepad at my desk, and I record the time and my activities for the previous hour every hour. Keep the notebook close at hand to ensure that you don't forget.

Step 2: Identify The Non-Productive Work

This process is really rather easy. Just one question: "Go through each of the repeating activities in your record one at a time. What would occur if you stopped performing them?

If "All hell breaks loose" was the response. Nothing should be altered. However, if you said, "Nothing would happen," You've made it. We all engage in actions that yield ZERO results. I refer to those pursuits as time wasters.

Step 3: Eliminate The Time-Wasters

Boom. I'm done now. Know how you spend your time. Sort the important duties in your life from the unimportant ones. And eliminate the pointless, time-wasting jobs. "That easy?" Yes. You regularly keep a log if you wish to be a really effective person. You are not required to keep a log for a full year. Instead, perform two two- to three-week periods per year. That's plenty to monitor your time usage and spot any new time wasters. A further advantage of such a straightforward activity is that it compels you to reflect on your everyday routine.

We frequently begin time-wasting behaviours and they become into habits. And it's challenging to overcome such poor habits if you aren't conscious of the needless activity. This practise has proven to be one of the most effective methods for increasing productivity. Start right away. Most likely, your activity log appears something like this:

• (Insert time) — I started maintaining a time journal after reading an article by Paul Foroux.

• (Insert time) — I put my phone away and returned to (whatever you were working on).

- Looked at the news, Facebook, and Instagram for (enter time). and watched videos on YouTube. (Be truthful to yourself. Things happen.
- I answered emails at (insert time).

Great. I'm glad to see you get going. Continue now for a further two weeks.

The Habits Of Unproductive People You Don’t Want To Copy

I study productivity because I am a non-productive person. I am, really. I get too much sleep. I speak way too much. I read excessively. All day long, I listen to music. I take in movies. I purchase technology that makes me a zombie.

Without my productivity method, I wouldn't accomplish anything. I certainly wouldn't have created this piece. However, all you see when you explore social media are images of extremely successful, wealthy, and healthy people. Is that a fact, though? I'm not sure. You cannot be productive constantly, I am certain of this. And giving up the unproductive habits we all have is a significant part of being productive.

The list of ten unproductive habits I learned to reduce or give up is provided below. Do you practise any of these behaviours? We're all occasionally unproductive, so don't stress. It might be time to alter, though, if you have five or more. Nobody wants to be a person who isn't productive, that much is certain.

Working Too Much

I can work for 12 or 13 hours nonstop on some days. I only pause to eat and exercise. And I'm capable of doing it for a few days. But there always seems to be a crash after a few days. Really big. I battle. I am unable to complete tasks. I don't even want to complete anything. This is bad. I thus learned to be more thoughtful about how much work I put in. At the peak of his day, Hemingway attempted to stop.

And that's my new objective. But that's challenging because we constantly want things immediately, now, now, fast, fast, quick, quick. Simply be aware of your deadlines, your work, and yourself. lacking a deadline? Take things easy; you'll need that energy for tough situations. Finally, remember to be patient.

Worrying Too Much

What if I lose everything? What if I get fired? What if I don't win her love? Suppose I develop cancer? Imagine if this aircraft crashes. What happens if I get blind? What if...?

You are burying your head so deep in the sand that you are blind to how narrow-minded that style of thinking is.

It's always, always about me. I am fully aware of it. The examples I gave above are all from my own experience. I once reigned supreme in the "what if" game. But let me tell you something: you are not going to pass away right now. overcoming oneself Give up worrying. And perform a useful action. You can learn how to stop worrying (I realise it's not that easy.)

Being Stubborn

We frequently interact with individuals. Do you ever question your decision to listen to this person? Also: "What does she know?" I'm not sure. perhaps more so than you do? We simply don't know until we hear what others have to say.

However, if you constantly believe that you are the best in the world, you will never give other people an opportunity. I believe everyone is obstinate. Some people are extremely stubborn, while others are just a bit.

I must admit that being stubborn is a positive quality. It's advantageous to disregard criticism and the opinions of others. However, being stubborn in a relationship is just plain annoying. That level of tenacity is undesirable. And by pure coincidence, relationships are the foundation of existence. also your professional life.

Therefore, by refusing to cooperate with others, you undermine the efforts of everyone else. Just keep it in mind. I try to constantly remind myself that being stubborn can be harmful. But occasionally it becomes so severe that I stop even listening to myself. But I continue to try.

Checking Things

What are you doing? “I was just checking Facebook.”

What are you “checking”?

Email? TMZ? CNN? NBA? NFL? Instagram? Twitter? Snapchat?

Checking serves no purpose. It may be a verb, but it doesn't really do anything. When I first started blogging, I frequently checked my metrics idly. Then I pondered: What did checking reveal?

Nothing. You merely take in knowledge. I aim to do as little "checking" as possible. I removed all news and social media apps from my phone because of this. My phone doesn't even have email. Otherwise, I constantly check it. I do not desire that. When I have time to respond to emails, that's when I want to check my email.

The habit of checking is one that you can never completely break. I continue to watch the NBA because I enjoy it. Choose no more than 1 or 2 vices that you genuinely enjoy. Remove everything else. In any case, you are not lacking anything.

Escaping Life

Before two years ago, if I felt worried, I'd say things like, "I need a drink." Or, "I need to take a trip."

And I chose to act as though I didn't have problems when they happened when they were too much for me to handle in my relationship or at work. I would occasionally take some time to discuss it. However, there are usually deeper problems at hand. I didn't like my work, my relationship, or the place I resided in back then. In general, I didn't enjoy my life.

Have I altered it? Nope. I attempted to run from my problems constantly. Avoiding issues provides you the strength to confront your mundane existence once more. But you and I both understand that issues persist until you snare them by the roots and put them out of their misery. I had a hard time learning that. These days, I handle issues before they balloon into major issues.

Saying Yes

Most individuals are reluctant to refuse. Perhaps you don't want to disappoint folks. Maybe the word "no" makes you uneasy. I'm not sure. Really doesn't matter. What counts is that you are living someone else's life if you continue to say yes.

Consider this. We all know it's true deep down. Even our own time is not under our control. Do you desire total control over your life? Say no to a lot of things and yes to the important things.

Not Writing Things Down

Yes, you do indeed possess an elephant's memory. Or perhaps you are so intelligent that you can recall everything.

WRONG. It's silly not to record your ideas, tasks, and other thoughts in writing. Why? Because relying on your memories consumes a lot of mental power. You can employ your brainpower for other tasks after you have everything in writing. like resolving issues. That genuinely helps your career and is helpful.

Even better is keeping a journal. However, I've discovered that not everyone like the concept of journaling. We'll just refer to it as "writing things down." What notes did you make while reading this article?

Being Hard On Yourself

"I suck!" No, you don't.

"Why?" You got out of bed this morning, right?

"Yeah." Congratulations. You survived this hard thing called LIFE. Be proud of yourself. Everything you do after getting out of bed is a win.

Neglecting Your Personal Education

"Woohoo! I finished college. Goodbye lame old books!"

No matter how long ago that was, if that was you, you DO stink. Who gains one insight before quitting forever? I'm not even sure how or why that notion got into our heads. I've always believed that education ends when you leave school. However, the reality is that when learning stops, your life ends.

Develop yourself. Take something in. Study a book. Take classes. watch movies Go somewhere or do it at home. It is irrelevant. Simply acquire new skills. You'll be more successful and enthusiastic about life.

Hating Rules

The greatest was reserved for last. I assume that most people despise rules. It begins when we are young. "Why must I perform this? Why must I perform that action? It's better for you because of that! That is the reason! But as adults, we don't have to abide by rules (apart from those established by the government, but you see what I mean).

"Rules are dumb!"

That's what I've always thought, too. I believed I was unique. However, I was a fool. The best thing about life is rules, in actuality. We would currently be pigs eating hotdogs if there were no restrictions.

The first rule of productivity is to establish rules. You are free to live a life without rules. Life, however, is not Fight Club. Rules genuinely assist us in problem solving and in making the most of life.

In his book Seducing Strangers, Mad Men co-producer Josh Weltman, who has worked as an advertising creative director for more than 25 years, said it best: "Solving an issue takes a bizarre combination of freedom and restraint. I have experience that whenever I hear advice like "Just have fun with it" or "Think outside the box," things are likely to become a huge waste of time.

Good news: You make up the rules.

One of my own rules, for instance, is to never complain. Another is to read and work out each day. And every evening, decide what would be your top priorities for the following day.

You have a system when you combine all of your productivity guidelines. Voila! A system also alters everything.

I count on my system to operate more shrewdly, competently, joyfully, and efficiently. It took me a while to realise that a system is beneficial, and it took me a while longer to really develop one, but the effort was worthwhile. I can now be productive because I get to. Not bad for someone who is not productive, huh?

This 30-Minute Evening Ritual Will Help You To Kick Life In The Ass.

It might be difficult to unwind and prepare for a restful night's sleep after a long day. Too frequently, I stay up late working. Additionally, I occasionally find myself reading or watching television.

And you are unable to fall asleep when you are ready. Your mind is racing with ideas that are distracting at this time of day. It's no secret that many individuals struggle to fall asleep. The National Sleep Foundation reports that 45% of Americans claim that, at least once over the previous seven days, their everyday activities were impacted by poor or insufficient sleep.

Why is tonight such a big deal? You might have a flawless morning routine, a well-organized schedule, and the determination to kill your day, but if you lack energy, you can't do anything.

I've tried a lot with morning and evening rituals over the past six months. What I've discovered is that creating a morning habit in your life is simple. They are nonetheless also simple to stop. When we are fatigued in the morning, we frequently revert to our unhelpful routines.

final outcome You fail, and life triumphs. In the end, you become uncontrollable, irrational, anxious, and generally unhappy. I've developed a nightly routine to aid in getting ready for some well-earned rest because of this. Get seven to nine hours of sleep every night. But all too frequently, life interferes, and we disregard common sense.

But I've discovered a great approach to give my evenings—and consequently, my life—more regularity with the help of the following evening habit.

From minute 0 to minute 10: Close The Day

I set aside 10 minutes every night to journal about my day. I sum up my accomplishments, my lessons learnt, and everything else important in a few phrases. That quick workout aids me in:

1. Keep in mind what I did (sounds stupid, but we forget most things we do).

2. Evaluate my performance to determine if I'm fulfilling all the requirements (like reading, working out, spending

time with my family, writing, talking to people I work with).

This activity is something Jim Rohn taught me. "You should review the recordings of your performance at the end of each day," he advises. The outcomes need to either encourage or challenge you.

It's easy: Before beginning a new day, end the previous day. Additionally, end each week before beginning a new one. Similar for every year and month. Sounds easy, doesn't it? One of those seemingly straightforward concepts that profoundly affects your life.

From minute 10 to minute 20: Review Tomorrow's Calendar

This is necessary. You want to know exactly what your day entails when you awake. Do you have any crucial appointments or phone calls? deadlines, perhaps? What tasks must you complete? When do you exercise? Do you have any urgent matters to attend to? When will you be addressing them?

This quick workout virtually eliminates all of my stress and worry. Most anxiety is caused by unresolved issues. We frequently worry about issues that aren't actually issues. However, you can unwind when you tell yourself: "I'm going to work on problem X from 10 to 11."

In the evening, you are helpless to accomplish anything. Please just go to bed. Save the problem-solving for the morning, when your mind will be more alert.

From minute 20 to minute 25: Prepare your outfit

Oh, you're so conceited. No, I don't want to put my intellect under unnecessary strain. Your brain is a muscle, you see. Additionally, your brain exhausts itself after a given number of decisions. As a result, the effectiveness of your decisions will decline.

It's referred to as Decision Fatigue. But since I'm going to bed so my brain can recharge in the evening, I'm not concerned about it. Making a few additional choices won't harm. Your productivity will suffer, though, if you make those few extra decisions in the morning. So why not plan your outfit in advance so you can save your limited morning brainpower?

From minute 25 till minute 30: Visualize

I already reviewed my calendar, so I am aware of how my day will proceed. Next, carefully imagine the following day.

This exercise is discussed by Charles Duhigg in his most recent book, Smarter Faster Better. According to Duhigg, those who are most productive have more detailed mental images of their days than the rest of us. I like to perform this exercise in the evening since it helps me recall what I've envisioned when I wake up in the morning.

The outcome is: NO MORE DOZING OFF.

You won't believe how many times in the past I would press the snooze button. In fact, I would snooze so frequently that my phone's alarm would just stop working. Hardcore snoozers are aware of what I'm referring to. You succeed if you hit snooze a lot. Contrarily, this is real. Losers don't snooze. But thanks to this 30-minute nighttime ritual, I'm no longer losing. I don't feel stressed before bed, and I wake up with clarity since I know exactly what needs to be done to make the day successful. And with this ceremony, I want to do that. If you want to better your life, investing 30 minutes of your evening seems like a pretty good investment.

So give it a shot this evening and judge for yourself. But don't be shocked if you awaken the following morning prepared to stomp life in the behind.

Why Disconnecting From The Internet Improves Your Focus

Life now is mostly good. You have constant access to the internet both inside and outside of your house. The entire world is at your fingertips thanks to your smartphone. Great, isn't that right? NOT. The majority of people rely on technology, rather than using it to their advantage.

Everything from apps to games to movies to articles to TV shows is made to maintain your interest. As a result, you lose several hours every week without even realising it. Your focus is all over the place but not where it should be. According to Seneca, a Stoic philosopher, "To be everywhere is to be nowhere."

Why does Netflix automatically begin the following episode in three, two, and one seconds? You may think, "Screw it, let's watch another episode," when it occurs. Likewise with YouTube. Why do you believe their recommendations are so excellent? They confine you inside. And every stuff falls under this. A "next" video, episode, article, game, round, or movie is ALWAYS available.

Funny enough, the majority of readers of these publications are aware of the negative effects of lack of attention. And a lot of study papers and books regarding the negative impacts of distractions have been published recently. Research specifically demonstrates that interruptions are linked to increased stress, frustration, time pressure, and effort.

Focused work is quite challenging. We're constantly preoccupied.

And you are not to blame. The majority of technology locks you in and taps into your reptilian brain, making you a consumer. Therefore, don't even consider opposing the internet or technology. You've probably given it a shot before. I won't ever spend hours browsing aimlessly. I see, right! What is effective? I recently blogged about how I developed a technique to overcome procrastination. One of that system's most important components is this:

DISCONNECT FROM THE INTERNET.

There is just one justification for doing that: There can never be too much of anything. even positive things

- Excessive exercise? You'll exhaust your training.

- Love in excess? You'll suffocate people.
- Overly much work? Burnout will set in.
- Overeating? You'll gain weight.
- A surplus of water? You'll pass away.

Why then do you use the internet so frequently? That was a question I asked myself two years ago. I was at a loss for words. I reasoned that since I use the internet in moderation along with everything else. I quickly discovered that there is no such thing as internet moderation. It resembles an unlimited smorgasbord. Even when you're already full, you continue to eat. And when you've overindulged, the regret will consume you whole.

The same applies to using the internet. It's incredibly alluring and satiating, and it's everywhere. So you give it your all. Snapchat, Facebook, Whatsapp, YouTube, etc. I'm all for getting rid of distractions. I also don't want to have a reclusive existence, though. I had to therefore find a reasonable midway ground. I discovered that making a small adjustment to how I feel about the internet solved the problem.

I went from "Always Connected" to "Always Disconnected."

In actuality, my phone's mobile data and wifi are both turned off by default. I only activate it when I require it. When I work, I run an app called SelfControl on my laptop (try FocusMe for Windows). The programme disables sites that are annoying. The benefit is that my connected apps, such as Evernote, DayOne, and Office 365, allow me to save my work in the cloud.

Being "always connected" is bad for your concentration and productivity. It is analogous to going to the gym. or cooking a meal. or spending a special evening with your significant other. You don't perform those actions continuously. You perform them for a half-hour, an hour, or several hours. Simply put, those things don't work well in excess.

Being off the internet has been quite beneficial to me. I no longer have the desire to check my phone, email, or the news 500 times every day.

And eventually, you begin to feel as though you are not missing anything. That makes your life feel more peaceful. I also do more than before, am less distracted, and have more time to devote to the activities that bring me joy. I also get more out of each day.

The internet is only a tool at the end of the day. Some of us, though, believe it to be everything. But I have a good feeling that I won't look back in the future and feel guilty for not using the internet more.

Can you picture it? You tell your loved ones as you lay dying, "I'm glad I watched so many YouTube FAIL compilations." Nope. You'll probably pause to think back on your time with loved ones or pals. or the experiences you had while travelling. or how much you cherished doing your job.

So stop being a jerk on the internet. You are just experiencing frustration as a result of it. Disconnect after reading this article. You may have withdrawal symptoms, such as repeatedly grasping your phone. Or continuously pressing the F key on your keyboard to access Facebook. However, I can assure you that disconnecting will enable you to DO more. And life is all about that.

The Single Biggest Reason Most People Procrastinate In Life

I've been a chronic procrastinator for the majority of my life. At age 16, I had my first summer job, and I made every effort to avoid working. I sold cellphone contracts to customers while working as an inside salesperson for a telecom business.

When you ended a call, the business's software would automatically call the following client. You would therefore be talking on the phone nonstop, but I managed to get around that. You were required to enter your activities into the system after each call. phrases like "Client is interested, but needs to talk to her grandchild about it." Yes, I did sell to a number of senior citizens (not proud of it).

I took a lot of time, as a professional procrastinator, to write a long account of the call. In response to my manager's question over the low volume of calls I receive each day, I responded, "If one of my teammates calls the customer, they know she had to chat to her grandchild. That's important knowledge, right?

I tried everything to delay the following call. While attending college and working on a marketing master's degree, I also put off things. I was never one to finish a project or prepare for an exam until the very last minute.

Even after I graduated and began working as a freelance marketing consultant, I slacked off. "I'm researching," I promised myself this time. I couldn't figure out why I always waited until the last minute to do things. I considered it a trait of my personality. Many of my acquaintances also expressed the same sentiment, asking: "Who wants to work? Let's enjoy a beer.

I used to think that working was something you only did because you needed the money and status: "Work is something you don't like to do." Sadly, a lot of us think that's the case. Fortunately, I stopped procrastinating this year. I wasn't transformed into a productivity machine by any sort of magical productivity hack or programme. I'm working harder and staying focused than ever. And compared to before, I'm happier with my work.

Do you wish to learn the truth? I'm at last engaged in a passion project.

I'm done now. Work is not at all unpleasant; I write every day of the week because I enjoy it. My past employment, the businesses I founded, and studying for schools I had no interest in were all things I disliked.

I used to believe that you procrastinate because you are ineffective at managing your time. Because of this, I've tried every productivity tip, method, and piece of software there is, but none of them are useful compared to doing worthwhile work. Do you wish to complete tasks? Do important things.

The topic of productivity hacks is often discussed. And rather frequently, individuals offer time-management advice as a solution. Time management is similar to speed reading, in a manner. Many of us desire to read books faster in order to finish more in less time. Yet why? I want to spend more time reading because I like to do it. It appears that we are simply interested in the results and wish to forgo doing the labour itself.

It's like Ryan Holiday writes in an article about speed reading: "If you find yourself wanting to speed up the reading process on a particular book, you may want to ask yourself, "Is this book any good?" Life is too short to read books you don't enjoy reading."

I believe you can use that saying to guide your life and work: Life is too short to spend it working at a job you hate. If you're not passionate about what you do, no matter how many productivity tricks you try, you won't generate more. If you frequently put off doing tasks, you might want to consider whether you are passionate about your profession.

Find something about which you are so fervently enthusiastic that you don't want to put it off for even a moment if the answer is no. Since everyone is aware that time is limited, why not act accordingly? Why squander time when you are aware that your time on this earth is finite?

"We all sorely complain of the shortness of time, and yet have much more than we know what to do with. Our lives are either spent in doing nothing at all, or in doing nothing to the purpose, or in doing nothing that we ought to do. We are always complaining that our days are few, and acting as though there would be no end of them."

– Lucius Annaeus Seneca

Do what you're good at, as well as what you're enthusiastic about, is something I really believe in. The ideal job is one that you enjoy doing and are skilled at; this is the sweet spot.

I don't mean to imply that productivity advice is pointless. I've even written about productivity strategies that increased my output. Doing important work is, in my opinion, the best antidote to procrastination.

Additionally, procrastination may indicate that you are working on unimportant tasks. Do not let putting off things become a habit. After all, putting off your hopes and goals is the worst kind of procrastination. Benjamin Franklin once said that time would not wait for you if you are waiting for the perfect moment. If you won't pay attention to me, do so to him.

This Ancient Habit Will Maximize Your Focus

I have worried a lot since I was a young child. My favourite subjects were my future, my health, and money. Which subject worries you the most? And please don't claim that you never worry or have any fears. Because being fearless indicates that you are a robot, not a human! Everyone spends time contemplating hypothetical scenarios. Because fear is exactly that. The philosopher Michel de Montaigne, who lived in the 16th century, best put it this way: "My life has been full of horrible catastrophes, most of which never happened."

We are all aware that fear is a protective emotion. But that simply isn't true anymore in the modern world. Fear these days is merely a thought in your mind. We are unable to concentrate on our objectives because our minds are so clouded by anxiety, worry, and stress. Living a fulfilled life, in my opinion, has nothing to do with your access to wealth or chances.

Knowing what you want and how to attain it are two key components. You should therefore maintain your focus each day. No goal will ever be attained without effort. I want to relate one old practise that has endured for this reason. This behaviour has repeatedly demonstrated its effectiveness.

The Power Of Having A Mantra

I'm not really spiritual. I think in luck and coincidence. I also don't think there is any sort of invisible spiritual force. I have a healthy dose of scepticism. I am a realist as well, though. What works is what I support. I never question religion or spirituality because it is effective for many people, which is why I do.

In actuality, I research religion, cultures, and many worldviews. And one lesson I took away from religion was the value of a mantra. Although most of us have heard of it, few of us actually have one or even actively practise it. What exactly is a mantra? This is a suitable definition I discovered online:

A sacred utterance known as a "mantra" is a numinous sound, syllable, word, phoneme, or combination of syllables in Sanskrit that its practitioners believe to have psychological and spiritual qualities.

Mantras have been around for ages (in many forms). They are present in Christianity, Taoism, Buddhism, and Hinduism. I've discovered that individuals from many walks of life utilise mantras to get over fear and sharpen their attention. It makes little difference who had the idea first. Its effectiveness is what matters.

My favorite example of someone who applies it is Floyd Mayweather.

Yes. The boxer. Perhaps Mayweather is a divisive figure that people either adore or detest. He is, nonetheless, regarded as the greatest boxer in history. Not among the very best. The finest. He has a 50-0 record. Furthermore, he was never even close to losing.

His formula for achievement? Absolutely, there is a tonne of skill. The man, however, also has an insane work ethic. And he has been practising since he was a young child.

I've been watching him for a long time. His cars and wealth are unimportant to me. I study his training videos to see if there is anything I can take away and use in my own life. Someone who achieves such types of accomplishments must act ethically. That cannot be disputed.

I came across something a few years back that at first glance appeared to be a promotion strategy. The same phrase was used frequently by Mayweather: "Hard work. Dedication."

It has the air of a tacky company tagline. While working on the heavy bag, speedball, pads, and even while running, he says that. He keeps saying the same thing again and over. occasionally in a different order

And I didn't begin employing my own mantra until I knew about Mayweather's. I've always assumed it's a technique used by yoga hipsters to achieve "Zen." Do you hear me muttering, "Hmmmn. Hmmmn. Hmmn" while seated on the floor with my legs crossed?

"Let's go."

That is my adage. Every morning when I wake up, I've conditioned myself to say that. It gives me lots of energy. As soon as I open my eyes, I say, "Let's go."

I've tried out a variety of mantras. especially the ones you use more frequently." But I've discovered that I'm not good at it. I don't do a lot of BS, and I'm fairly direct. Something succinct and potent is what I favour. I say that both before I start working and when I first wake up. or whenever I want to begin working out. "Let's go."

Test it out. For me, it works incredibly well because it shifts my mindset from contemplation to action. I attempt to induce a change in state, particularly during times when I feel terrified or helpless in life. You've heard the expression, "The only way out is through"? I think that's accurate. And you need to take action if you want to move forward.

After you start using your Mantra, you get into a worry-free zone.

One of the best things I've discovered for personal development is this. Everyone should use a mantra, in my opinion. All you have to do is choose a slogan that gets you focused and alters your mood. Try it out right away.

But I don't think so!

"Just speaking three words won't help you with genuine difficulties," the pessimists assert. What will be of assistance, I ask those people? In your own misery, drowning? being rendered mute? Taking no action at all? Complaining? Do you feel resentful of life?

Never. We are all aware that life is too short to waste time thinking about unimportant matters. And take action if something horrible does happen to you.

How To Focus Better: Manage Your Attention (not your time)

How many uninterrupted minutes do you typically work in a day? 10, 20, or even fifty minutes? Just take a look at your life if you think that sounds depressing. Most of us are unable to remain quiet for longer than ten minutes.

It is tough to find time to concentrate on yourself and your work because we are all so connected. Each day, some of us receive hundreds of notifications and texts. You find yourself responding to emails here, Whatsapp messages there, conversations with friends on Slack, and conversations with coworkers. The majority of people's days are spent responding to notifications. You could say that they are holding you captive.

It makes sense then that so many of us wonder, "How do I focus better?"

I routinely ask new readers to my email about their difficulties. And the majority of those who respond bring up a subject connected to focus. In fact, when I polled readers of my newsletter, 28% responded that maintaining concentration and managing their time was their toughest issue. Here are just a couple of reader comments that I received:

- "Trying to maintain concentrate on my responsibilities is my biggest problem in life and in my career. When I'm at work, my thoughts always begin to stray to unimportant matters.

- "How can we define what to genuinely focus on?" is my toughest issue.

These thoughts have also crossed my head in the past. You know what I discovered? Distractions are not a first-world issue for the twenty-first century. Life has always been filled with distractions. Your smartphone, YouTube, online shopping, Instagram, or anything else you wish to hold responsible for your lack of concentration has nothing to do with it. It is in our nature. We enjoy staying occupied.

Beware the barrenness of a busy existence, Socrates, one of the founders of Western philosophy, cautioned us 2400 years ago.

Being overly busy is not a good thing. because distractions and busyness go hand in hand. No distractions, please. Go to the forest. But that isn't how life functions. Life in the modern day is also too good. There is never a time when a fresh distraction won't appear, according to Seneca, one of the most well-known Stoic thinkers.

Distractions are always present. You should therefore practise attention management. Not now, sir. Because most individuals make that error. We misjudge our ability to manage time. But managing time is impossible. Your focus is the only thing you have control over.

And never forget: Your life's quality is determined by your focus. Lack of focus results in loss of attentional control. And being powerless leads to frustration. We are all aware of what frustration can do. Begin controlling your focus. Not now, sir.

Part II
Improving Productivity

Smartphones Harm Your Productivity More Than You Think

I assure you that the device you are using to read this post is not a friend of yours. Even if you're reading this on a computer or laptop, I have one question for you: How significant is your gadget to you?

When I recently read a strange statistic, I was astounded. 37.4 percent of participants in a study by the universities of Würzburg and Nottingham Trent regarded their phones as more or equally essential to them than their closest friends.

Weirdoes. What's wrong with humans, for real? Even more bizarrely, 29.4% of those weirdos claimed that their smartphone was just as essential to them as their parents, if not more so. Or am I just flawed in some way? Am I just an old-fashioned bookworm who appreciates just a select group of close friends and family members and spends his days reading?

I'm not kidding, you see. Smartphones pose a threat. Because they alter your behaviour rather than because they could lead to tension, worry, or even depression. We appear to be unable to concentrate on anything for longer than five seconds. Why? We can't, though, because our smartphone never stops beeping.

You're always receiving notifications on things that don't matter, not because people are calling you (although it seems like people are afraid to call these days, but that's another discussion).

Change Your Smartphone Behavior

Another finding from the same study is as follows: "Researchers asked individuals to take a concentration test under four distinct conditions: with their smartphone in their pocket, at their desk, locked in a drawer, and removed from the room entirely."

The test scores were lowest when the smartphone was on the desk, but test performance improved with each additional layer of separation between individuals and their smartphones. When phones were taken out of the room, test outcomes were overall 26% better. Yes, it is only a study. You also don't have to take everything you read at face value. But I can speak from experience on this. I've dramatically changed my smartphone usage habits during the past two years. In particular: • I've only allowed notifications for calls and messages.

I only consume music, paid journalism, articles from specific authors I follow, podcasts, YouTube videos (mostly to learn, but also for entertainment because I'm not a robot), books, and audiobooks on it. I've removed myself from all Whatsapp groups aside from one with my closest friends. I've removed all news apps.

• The rest of the time, I use my phone to make calls, send texts, and capture pictures and videos.

Additionally, I no longer reply to notifications right away. That doesn't imply that I don't appreciate other individuals trying to get in touch with me. It implies that I don't want to be a phone's servant. My phone is in my hands.

The situation is reversed for the majority of us. My thoughts used to be governed by Facebook, Instagram, Apple, Google, and other platforms. The only way to get away from such jerks is to cut yourself off and run to the woods, so obviously they still do. That is not practical.

My phone is great. I don't require it though.

Since I started utilising my smartphone in the manner described above, the results have been fantastic. I completed more tasks in the last two years than at any other time. I also still find time to go to the gym every day, hang out with my friends, eat supper with my family, and see my girlfriend. The same 24 hours are available to you and I.

The way you use those 1440 minutes each day will make a difference. Sincerity be damned, I believe I still have a lot to learn about efficacy. No one ever reaches their maximum output. It also doesn't matter whether you're the world's most productive person.

It's up to you how you want to spend your time. But please don't tell me you don't want to increase your productivity by 26% by altering just one insignificant aspect of your life: how you use your smartphone.

And if you're wondering why nobody is advising you to get rid of that thing, just remember that they're only after your money. Additionally, those on social media who assert that their smartphone serves as their primary business tool are engaging in the same behaviour. You guessed it, your smartphone, is what they need you to use to access their material.

Additionally, Apple would never advise us to avoid purchasing the next iPhone because it will kill our productivity. Of course not, despite what they attempt to convince you of. Additionally, smartphones unquestionably increase productivity. Most likely, your phone is where you found my articles. That's fantastic. I read a lot of books and articles on my phone as well. However, both you and I utilise the gadget to educate ourselves, which is always a good thing.

We are not as intelligent as those who create phones and apps. Their only objective is to seduce you. Realizing that is beneficial, in my opinion. I constantly try to remind myself that I should not rely too heavily on my smartphone because my attention is more important than my productivity. It's time to take back your focus. and reclaim your life as a result. It is worthwhile.

How Perfectionism Is Destroying Your Productivity

Do you frequently fear that you performed poorly? Do you frequently reflect about the things you do and say? Are you reluctant to acknowledge your errors? Do you get the shits when you get rejected?

In that case, you face serious risks. I don't strive for perfection myself. I try to convince myself that, at least. You probably try to convince yourself of that as well. In actuality, those who refuse to acknowledge it are the worst. But here's the thing: If you're a perfectionist, all you're doing is procrastinating under a disguise. It is comparable to someone who is completely inactive due to laziness. You don't trust me? Let's look at it. a stickler for detail

Never makes a mistake, always requires more time, and waits for the appropriate time.

However, life and business are ultimately about results. Results count. And if you strive for perfection, you could one day succeed. But the real query is: When? How much will it cost? Particularly, studies demonstrate a strong correlation between depression and low self-esteem and perfectionism.

“Perfectionists are their own devils.” —Jack Kirby

Is perfectionism's price truly worth it? Perfectionism, in my experience, is merely another way to put off doing something. Doubt starts to sneak into your head when you worry about making mistakes all the time. And that leads to uncertainty. Two varieties of perfectionists exist:

1. The one that is always late. You want to accomplish something, but as soon as you begin, you begin to doubt yourself. "I don't think I can do it," you say. hence, you never begin.

2. The one who begins but sets unreasonable criteria. You chose a target. You put forth a lot of effort (maybe too hard). But because you have such high expectations for yourself, you constantly fall short.

The following can result from any scenario: Depression, anxiety, concern, and Type A behaviour.

We would want to stay away from these things. Researchers on worry, procrastination, and perfectionism Joachim Stöber and Jutta Joormann write: "The combination of worry over mistakes and procrastination may be an important role in the maintenance of worry. On the one hand, it might increase current threats if no action is made to combat them. On the other hand, because initially manageable problems will build up, generating an excess of problems that may ultimately be intractable, it may intensify current risks or even develop new ones.

The biggest trap for us is the sense of helplessness. Due to the fact that what do we do when we feel helpless? Yes, we give up. Simply review the research on learned helplessness.

Perfectionism isn't always a terrible thing, though. In fact, according to several studies, perfectionism is associated with higher achievement. However, that is not the issue at hand.

Of sure, you achieve more if you have higher standards and better ambitions. Without a question, having a tendency for perfection can be beneficial. But as we are all aware, life is not all about accomplishing your goals. It is more important HOW we achieve our objectives and dreams.

"How can we beat the nasty side of procrastination and perfectionism?"

We've discussed the links between perfectionism and procrastination as well as the potential negative effects of both. But what is the answer? I came upon a fascinating research by Gordon L. Flett and his associates that discusses the relationship between perfectionism and learnt resourcefulness. They contend that acquired ingenuity can serve as a mediator. I therefore began researching acquired resourcefulness. And this is what I discovered in a Michael Rosenbaum article: The behavioural repertoire required for both regressive and reformative self-control is referred to as "learned resourcefulness. Using problem-solving techniques, self-regulating one's emotional and cognitive reactions in high-stress situations, and postponing immediate satisfaction in favour of future, more significant benefits are all part of this repertory. You need to develop learned resourcefulness if you want to cease sabotaging your own efforts.

Consider the antithesis of a perfectionist: a lame-duck.

If you're a lazy, not much matters to you. Your motto is good enough. You also lack any ambition at all. That kind of mentality won't get you anyplace. The finest way to explain it was by American author Cormac McCarthy: "It's like a lot of things, remarked the smith. If you get even one thing wrong, it's better to get everything wrong.

Slackness is a "I don't care" attitude. However, you need to care if you want to change your life. Finding a balance between your perfectionistic tendencies, which push you, and your slacker-like calm and trained resourcefulness is what you want to do. I therefore managed to strike a balance between perfectionism and laziness.

Do excellent job like a perfectionist, but don't focus on your goals too much like a lazy. And finally, add this to it:

Goals might be beneficial, but they can also have the opposite effect. For this reason, you should rely on systems. And when sh*t falls out, use your problem-solving abilities to resolve the situation.

The sweet spot, in my opinion, is when you just modify or deal with the issue rather than beating yourself up when you make a mistake or fail yourself.

• Steer clear of the phrase that perfectionists love to use: "OMG, this is the worst thing ever!"

• Steer clear of the lazy person's go-to phrase, "I don't care."

But you respond, "I've got this," instead.

What then is your present problem? You've got this, so I don't even need to ask.

How To Read 100 Books A Year

Do you have a growing list of books to read? Have you purchased any books that you haven't read? It might be time to check off more books this year than ever before. You're not the only one who reads less than they would like to. I only read five novels in 2014, according to my Goodreads page, which I spotted a year ago. That epiphany annoyed me.

I adore reading, but ever since I left college in 2011, I've been reading less books each year. My life and career prevented me from reading as much as I would have liked. Why would one read 100 books in a year? You read because you want to gain knowledge from the experiences of others. The best quote is from Otto von Bismarck: "Fools learn from experience. I favour picking up knowledge from other people's mistakes.

You must educate yourself if you want to succeed in this world, and reading is the best way to educate yourself. This is the procedure.

1. Buy In Bulk

If you're reading this, I'll assume you have both the money and the time necessary to purchase and read books. Anyone can find the time. Find a way to make or save money if you don't have any. Erasmus, a Renaissance man from the Netherlands, famously remarked, "When I have a little money, I buy books; and if I have any left over, I buy food and clothing."

Rest certain that the time and money you invest in reading are worthwhile. There isn't a better investment in my opinion. Reading books is not necessary for them to be a waste of money. You must purchase more books if you wish to read more. Others fail to grasp it. They shell out $200 on brand-new sneakers, but they think it's absurd to order 20 books from Amazon.

The concept is straightforward: Having more books in your home will give you more options, which will encourage you to read more. This is why: The majority of the books you read are not pre-planned. You don't sit down in January and decide, "I'll read this book the first week of June."

When you finish a book, you determine what to read next after checking your inventory. You'll squander time reading reviews for hours if you spend too much time debating which book to read next.

For instance, the majority of individuals who wish to begin practising stoicism ask me which author—Seneca, Marcus Aurelius, or Epictetus—they should study first. Buy each one. Read each one. Having a collection of books keeps things moving. There is also never a good reason not to read.

2. A(always) B(e) R(eading)

The play/movie Glengarry Glen Ross: Always Be Closing may be where you first heard the word "ABC." That is a motto that many business owners and salespeople follow.

My personal mantra is "Always Be Reading." On weekdays, I read for at least an hour, and on weekends and holidays, I read much more. Find a method to fit reading into your schedule and circumstances. Make no such justifications as being too tired or busy. Always Be Reading means you should read while doing the following: riding the train, nursing your child, eating, seeing the doctor, and working.

And last but not least, read while everyone else is idly watching the news or opening Facebook for the 113th time today.

You'll read more than 100 novels in a year if you do that. How? Read on. Most readers finish 50 pages in one hour. You'll read 26,000 pages a year if you read for 10 hours a week. Say you read 250 pages per book on average: You will read 104 books in this scenario in a calendar year.

At that rate, you'll read at least 100 novels in a year—even if you take a two-week hiatus. That represents a good return on the time you spent. How profitable is reading the news? Although I'm not certain, it must be bad.

3. Read Relevant Books Only

Have you ever read a book that everyone says is incredible but you just don't grasp it? I wouldn't go so far as to claim that all books are bad because they take a lot of effort to write and edit.

But not everyone will enjoy every book. Even though a book is a best-seller, you could not enjoy the writing. Or perhaps now isn't the best moment to read a book. Whatever the case, if you find it difficult to turn the pages, put the book away and pick up something that will thrill you enough to tear the pages.

Read novels that are relevant to your current situation. There is a book for just about anything you can imagine. People have been writing books for 2000 years, and many of them have been in your position—struggling teenagers, ambitious artists, broke business owners, new parents, etc. Spending time reading about topics you have no interest in is a waste of time.

Choose books that are linked to your profession or passion instead. Read biographies of people you respect. If a book has no value to you, don't read it just because it's a best-seller or classic.

4. Read Multiple Books Simultaneously

There are no restrictions when it comes to reading, so do as you choose. I occasionally read five books at once. In the morning, I might read 50 pages of one book, and in the afternoon, I might read another book.

That's the way I like it. Some people prefer to finish reading a book before moving on to something else. If you're reading anything challenging, you might want to save your evening reading for something simpler. Since biographies are like stories, I enjoy reading them before bed. Evening reading of fiction is also effective.

With a highlighter and a pen, I don't want to read a book about investing in bed. My mind is racing with all the new information I'm learning, so if I do that, I won't fall asleep until three in the morning.

5. Retain The Knowledge

Knowledge is only useful if it is put to use. You need a method that aids in memory retention if you want to do that. What I do is as follows:

- When reading a book, use a pen to highlight key passages and write notes in the margins. Be careful not to over-highlight when reading on a digital device. You shouldn't highlight anything you find even remotely intriguing just because it's so simple. Keep the highlighting to only the "aha" moments.

- Fold the top or bottom corner of the paper if you are reading something you want to remember for sure. Take a picture and save it in your preferred note-taking programme for readers who use digital devices.

- After finishing the book, skim your notes on the pages with the folds.

- What the book is about and any advise the author offers should be noted in your own words (using note-taking software or a real notepad).

- The quotes that really resonate with you should be copied.

The goal is to aid you in processing the information so you may use it later, not to duplicate the book verbatim. Read as much as you can, but remember to put what you've learned into practise because that is ultimately what matters. Make sure you gain anything from your extensive reading time.

Take A Vacation: It Boosts Your Productivity And Reduces Stress

When your phone runs out of power, you recharge it. When your tank is empty, you fill it up again. You occasionally neglect to do the same for your body (and the brain that resides inside of it), which is your most valuable possession. You are working, whether you enjoy what you do, are between jobs, or have a job you detest. Living is a work as well. A challenging one, in fact.

Even just getting out of bed in the morning might be difficult. I'm not even mentioning all the obligations we have. Why then do you add to the difficulty of your life by refusing to take a break to rejuvenate? I'm not referring about your weekends that are jam-packed with events or your vacations when you work more than you unwind.

No, that kind of "spare time" is not productive. I'm referring to taking a break in order to recharge so that you can continue working hard. Life is about working hard, in my opinion. The best way to put it is how Voltaire said it: "As I become older, I find employment more and more vital. In the long term, it replaces life's illusions and turns into the greatest of pleasures.

Rest eases tension. increases productivity and creativity.

A vacation, according to scientific study, reduces perceived job stress and burnout. That is a really good reason to take a few days off, in my opinion. There's more, though. I'm constantly interested in productivity, as you may know. My concern is whether taking a break or going on vacation will result in me accomplishing more when I return. The answer is yes, but there is a crucial point to remember. But before, a brief digression What does the phrase "get more done" mean? Time has little to do with getting things done; even if you work longer hours, you might not accomplish more.

In reality, studies show that in general, working longer hours results in less productivity. Why? If we have extra time, we tend to waste it. It is as easy as telling someone they have a year to write an article. How would you respond? Do you procrastinate?

What if I were to inform you that you only have two hours? You instantly consider how to compose this post as soon as possible. In a sense, having more days off and fewer days at work compels you to use your time more wisely. According to research, taking a vacation alone won't increase your productivity, but having more days off will make you more motivated to do more tasks in a shorter amount of time.

And in that case, you, your company, or your employment stand to gain. After taking a short break to rest, refuel, and spend time with friends or family, you return to work more productive. Sounds fantastic. There's a catch, though. The advantages disappear if your trip is stressful. Have you ever seen Chevy Chase in National Lampoon's Vacation? My family's holidays were spent this way. Very bad.

Therefore, try to limit your holiday's stress. Otherwise, you'll have lost a wonderful chance to unwind and increase your overall productivity. Here are a few pointers that may be useful.

1. If You're A Planner, PLAN

One of my buddies is incredibly organised. When he is on vacation, he enjoys making detailed day plans and itineraries. In contrast, I am.

He said, "I'm going to mimic your style and simply go with the flow," when we went on a trip a few years ago. "Perfect," I murmured. I slept till ten in the morning on the first day. In actuality, he spent the entire morning making a routine after waking up early and being anxious over not having one.

Avoid attempting to be someone you are not. Simply do it if you like to organise your vacation. You're on vacation, so try to be adaptable.

2. Make A Daily Movie

It's original, and it's a wonderful memory for the future. Additionally, concentrating on the act of filming will require you to pay attention to a particular subject. By doing so, you will be more present and less worried about things at home.

Do not, however, record nonstop. You won't be there if you don't. A smartphone is all you require. Simply use your phone to record content and modify it there. Bring a decent camera and a laptop if you're more interested in video.

3. Read A LOT

Bill Gates is renowned for being an avid reader. He is renowned for his "Think Weeks," during which he does nothing but read and reflect.

He has recently started writing posts frequently about the novels he is reading this summer. If you're looking for some ideas, check out his website. Personally, I enjoy spending my vacation days reading nonstop. Reading helps you think more clearly, slows down time, and is healthy for your brain.

4. Get Bored

Boredom is one of my favourite methods for coming up with fresh ideas. Because of the distractions, it sounds simpler than it is. I used to do everything possible to avoid becoming bored, including watching TV, going out, and browsing Facebook. But did you realise that you may capitalise on boredom?

Simply give in to boredom and let your mind wander instead of giving in to distractions. In fact, Andy Warhol, one of my all-time favourite painters, embraced ennui. You can tell by the dull movies he produced or the allusions to boredom he made in The Philosophy Of Andy Warhol.

I just stop trying to be creative whenever it happens. Absolutely nothing. Try it out once. It's a wonderful plan; perhaps you'll think of the next big thing in your sector. Take breaks are never a smart idea. We invent a variety of justifications, including:

- "I just need to finish this project."
- "My boss will never accept it."
- "People will think I'm lazy."

- “I don’t have time.”
- “Money never sleeps.”

Yes, I have also been there. But which would you prefer: to labour nonstop and become exhausted? Or rest up before you get tired? Yes, life is long; thus, think long term. That being said, even if I'm not yet exhausted, it's time for me to take a rest. Therefore, when I return on August 1 with a fresh post, I'll see you again. Take it easy until then because I will undoubtedly.

P.S. I struggled for years to pay for vacations. Have a staycation if you find yourself in the same situation. The advice from above is still valid.

Eliminate Mindless Browsing

Everybody has days when they feel unproductive or like they accomplished nothing. The likelihood is that interruptions and multitasking are the cause of your perceived lack of productivity.

Context switching occurs when you multitask while attending a meeting, such as by sending an email, texting a buddy, and browsing Facebook. Gloria Mark of the University of California, Irvine conducted study that revealed that typically takes 25 minutes to get back to the original job following an interruption. We are stopped frequently, so this soon mounts up, and before you know it, you feel as though you accomplished nothing that day.

Sociologist Clifford Nass of Stanford University has studied the effects of multitasking and discovered that those who do so are "suckers for irrelevancy." We multitask because we are addicted to alerts' addictive distractions.

We are powerless to stop ourselves; we must examine the notification to determine who or what is requesting our attention. We experience a surge that causes dopamine to be released every time a notification appears on our screens. One of the body's happy neurotransmitters, dopamine regulates the brain's "pleasure" systems and induces happiness. This happy feeling is compulsive, leading us to seek out activities that release dopamine. You may consider things like food, sex, narcotics, and screen notifications.

Dopamine may give us a buzz, but it also wears us out. Because of this, even though you had a productive day, you still felt fatigued at the end of it. We need to break this cycle because it is damaging.

The Fix: Eliminate Browsing

Taking charge of your day is a simple way to be more productive. The biggest detriment to your productivity is browsing. It completely destroys it. Everybody has experienced a time dilation when browsing. "What?! I was SILENT for two hours. In fact, we do this at work as well. Take charge of your time and focus. Do something worthwhile, that is the point. Be mindful of your time. Spend money in a way that will make your life better.

20 Things That Will Make You More Productive Than Ever

For me, the past three years have been enormous. I moved nations, acquired an apartment and a small office building, spent a lot of time with my family and friends, maintained a healthy lifestyle, and worked out at least four times each week. I've accomplished more than ever.

Your overall productivity is determined by a number of factors. Without the proper mentality, tools, apps, or hacks won't help you be more productive since productivity is a way of life. It's all about getting the job done quickly, efficiently, and without wasting any time. I believe that productivity and happiness are interrelated. I consider inaction to be misery.

I want to offer 20 activities I've engaged in over the past three years that have increased my productivity (in no particular order).

1. Always Get Right to the Point

There is a lot of junk and things that matters in life, as there is with everything else. Small talk, idle chatter, waiting, postponing, and remaining silent are all pointless. You must get right into the activity if you want to accomplish anything.

2. Jot down all of your ideas and thoughts.

We have Random Access Memory, which is a feature of computers (RAM). Your human RAM holds pertinent, recent data. But you have a finite amount of RAM. Older information you have stored will be erased when it fills up to create way for new data. To free up RAM and increase mental capacity, you should jot down your ideas. It's still valuable even if you never look at that note once more.

3. Say No When it comes to work, I decline everything that doesn't advance my objectives and principles. There are constantly enough opportunities since we live in a world of abundance. I refuse anything in my personal life that doesn't excite me. I always respond with a firm NO when I have a neutral opinion. That stops me from wasting time on things I don't find exciting.

4. Break for five minutes every 30 to 45 minutes.

You can go around, stretch your back, and sip some water. However, it's more crucial that you look away from your task. You might have fresh ideas when you get back to your desk. You might also ask yourself, "WHAT AM I DOING?" And quit before you completely waste your time.

5. Get Rid of All Distractions Willpower is overrated. Eliminate any distractions if there are any. One of my pals is dependent on the news. I advised him to turn off his television, remove his news applications, and restrict access to news websites on his laptop. He let me know that he is finally establishing a business two weeks later. Don't assume your diversions won't affect you. Take them out.

6. Refrain from Clutter

A cluttered brain results from a cluttered life. And you can't accomplish anything when your mind is cluttered. I favour a straightforward working and living environment. a laptop, a notebook, and a desk. Ensure simplicity. No fluff is necessary for you.

7. Concentrate on One Thing Some Days

Try to complete as much of the same task on one day as possible if you have repeating duties. The other days of the week I use for my other projects and enterprises; I publish a couple of blog entries on one of those days. I switch off my phone and only write while I'm writing. Nothing else interferes.

8. Reduce Your Information Consumption

You don't have to read 5000 productivity articles. Try it if you find any relevant information. Don't look any further. Not usually, more is better. You only have so much processing capacity. Start producing instead than consuming.

9. Establish routines

Making decisions taxed your head. And routines do away with making choices. Thus, there will be an increase in brainpower. Routines are effective; they are not OCD. Apply them.

10. Avoid multitasking

Context switching is what happens when you multitask while you're in a meeting, such as sending an email, texting a friend, and checking Facebook. Gloria Mark of the University of California, Irvine conducted study that revealed that typically takes 25 minutes to get back to the original job following an interruption. It's a waste of time to do that.

11. Review Email Twice Daily

A dopamine high occurs each time you check your email. I understand it; the majority of us are addicted, and checking email feels good. Dopamine may give you a buzz, but it also wears you out. Because of this, even though you had a productive day, you still felt fatigued at the end of it.

Turn off notifications and only check your email twice each day at predetermined times to reduce that.

12. Don't use your smartphone for the first hour of the day.

The main purpose of a smartphone is to bother you. But during the first hour of your day, avoid being interrupted by other people or apps. Spend the first hour contemplating the day that lies ahead, reading a book, taking in your breakfast, coffee, or tea.

13. Prepare for tomorrow

I take five minutes every night before I go to sleep to establish my priorities (typically three to four) for the following day. When I wake up, I have better clarity as a result. If I don't engage in this exercise, I find that I waste time. Going with the flow is cool. The only issue is that I don't want to be a dog that aimlessly pursues moving vehicles.

14. Reduce Your Need for "Thinking"

when someone declares, "I'm thinking." They imply worrying through thought. Do not overthink. Simply DO it and watch what occurs. Continue if you like what you see. If not, change your course.

15. Workout

Food, water, housing, relationships, and exercise are a few things that are essential to life. You are unable to function adequately without this material. According to scientific studies, daily exercise can improve your mood, intelligence, and energy.

16. Laugh A Little Comedy is a great stress reliever. Stress is not good if you want to maintain your productivity. Therefore, try to raise your mouth's corners as much as you can.

17. Avoid Attending Meetings

For those who work for corporations, this is a challenging one. Some businesses have a culture of meetings. Meetings are scheduled merely to appear important or to put off doing the actual task. For the love of God, QUIT.

18. Is That Actually Required?

As often as you can, ask yourself that question. You'll discover that your response is frequently "Nope." Why then take useless actions?

19. Press Reset if you're having a gloomy day.

You might mess up, someone might get upset with you—stuff happens. Don't let it bring you down. Spend some time alone and do something relaxing like walk or listen to music. Don't let your day pass you by; try to get back on course. Work Hard

Yes, it is simpler to talk about work than to really perform it. Anyone can complete it. But you can't be everyone, can you? You are a monster of production. Act accordingly.

I could not be productive in the least without these 20 things. You've probably noticed that I avoid specifics like the tools and programmes I use. That material doesn't seem to matter to me. It involves setting up a productive mindset and surroundings that allow you to flourish. I merely care about finishing tasks quickly and without stress. That makes working much more enjoyable and gratifying.

Here's Why Time Off Work Actually IMPROVES Your Work and Life

What do you do if you're worn out or overburdened? Do you persevere? Alternatively, do you take a break? In the past, I believed that you should always persevere despite all odds. I still hold that viewpoint now about life in general. You must continue to look after your family and yourself.

One of the most potent motivators in life is a sense of responsibility. I'm not, however, referring about a lack of drive. I refer to taking time off from work. But taking time off is still strongly stigmatised. Some believe it's only for losers. Others believe it's about running away from your job. After all, "Why even need a break if you love your work and life?" Well said, clever ass. Here's why taking time off actually BENEFITS your job and personal life.

In his book Elastic, physicist Leonard Mlodinow—who also wrote two books with Stephen Hawking—recently presented scientific study on vacationing. He provides evidence that taking time off from work is beneficial to our wellbeing: "Though some may consider "doing nothing" unproductive, a lack of downtime is detrimental to our wellbeing, because idle time allows our default network to make sense of what we've previously experienced or learned."

Short-term focused individuals are those who never take time off to do nothing. "I must now achieve my objectives!" However, short-term thinking continues to hinder your long-term growth and development. What happens if you push through work and become exhausted? In most cases, you get worse results and work less efficiently. Sometimes you can sink into depression, which will cause you to fall even more behind.

Prevent Rather Than Cure

One of the book's major cliches is this. But how frequently do we actually avoid problems? We instead choose to "deal with it later" and keep our heads down. a poor strategy It is far preferable to avoid burnout or a decline in general work performance.

The greatest way to avoid exhaustion and stress, according to self-help pioneer Dale Carnegie, author of How to Stop Worrying and Start Living, is to rest frequently. Don't get exhausted before you rest.

So plan your vacations wisely throughout the year. That's what I just did too, and as a result, I gained 5 advantages:

1. You Can Check Whether You Did The Right Things

At work, I know two modes:

1. Execution
2. Thinking

When you are in execution mode, you can work continuously for several hours, days, or even months. I actually know individuals who have been in execution mode for a long time. They never stopped to pause or reflect on their work. Result? a crisis in midlife. or young people going through a quarter-life crisis.

That is what you get when you focus on the task at hand and act quickly. You might see outcomes. However, are those outcomes what you WANT? You have more inner dialogue when you take time off from job. However, you don't when you execute. One of the most significant advantages of doing nothing is that. Yes, you could end up behind on your tasks. Who is to care? Would you rather pursue a job with only one goal in mind?

In order to properly reflect, I need at least ten days off. I've been alternating between execution and thinking mode for the first five days. If you're used to working, it's challenging to adapt to thinking and doing nothing. But when I take a longer sabbatical, I always discover something new about myself. I enjoy reading a lot. I've read five books in the last two weeks. I didn't write anything, though. I also didn't write much in my journal.

Reading, watching documentaries, conversing with friends, and daydreaming are all acceptable activities. that sort of thing. It doesn't cost a lot either. But the payoff is substantial. I feel better now, have more energy, and am eager to resume work. That was the following lesson I discovered.

2. You Get To Process Your Ideas

You may not be aware of many of the activities your brain does. Processing of thoughts by our brains is one subconsciously occurring activity. I'm sure everyone has had ideas that were never carried out. How many people have you encountered who asserted to be the creators of Facebook, Instagram, or any other novel concept? I once spoke with a man who claimed to be the inventor of the electric bicycle. Has he used it in any way? No. He now buys trash on Alibaba and sells it door-to-door to companies. We're all thinking. not just business concepts.

- "I want to paint the walls of the house."
- "I'd like to take a car from NYC to LA."
- "I'd like to publish a book."

Great ideas, all of them. However, how are you going to use them? Not even execution is on my mind. Every concept needs to be processed. Are the concepts sound? Is that what I actually want to do? That involves thinking once more. Without thinking things through beforehand, you frequently squander time in the long run. Naturally, you can never completely avoid that. But by giving your thoughts some thought now, you can spare your future self a lot of suffering, anxiety, and even expense.

3. You Can Consume More Art

Describe art. anything that stimulates thought. a great book, poetry, essay, song, movie, painting, sculpture, etc. Anything may be art. There is no official definition of what constitutes art.

Art is a huge source of inspiration for me. Without it, I'm not sure what life would be like. Yes, there is artwork there as well. Just read Fahrenheit 451 or see Equilibrium on the big screen. The greatest benefit of art is that it elevates your mood. And you're happy when you're in a good mood. Just avoid consuming unnecessary crap. begin with timeless works. Pay attention to Whitney Houston, Marvin Gaye, and Bob Dylan. watch films by Francis Ford Coppola and Alfred Hitchcock. Read Ralph Ellison, Harper Lee, and Ernest Hemingway. Visiting the British Museum Look into Andy Warhol. You will be moved by their art, just like many others have been. And that will make your life better.

4. You Can Focus On Other Important Things (that are not work related)

What more can you tell me about yourself? What comes to mind when I pose that query to you? The majority of us begin by introducing ourselves as "I'm an accountant at company X." You are virtually forced to identify yourself with your employment in today's world. However, you are not your work. You are your loved ones, friends, pastimes, and passions, and you also have a job. Additionally, work is crucial. But the other things are as well.

Thus, you should never ignore the other vital aspects of your life. Develop your bonds with your loved ones and close pals. Combine your efforts. Take a family vacation. Join your friends for a mountain bike ride. Display initiative. Why aren't YOU doing action if no one else in your family or circle of friends is? By putting effort into your connections, you create shared memories. Your relationships will only get stronger as a result.

In addition, pay attention to you. What interests you? What are you interested in learning more about? What did you want to accomplish? Take those actions.

5. Resting Gets Boring. Quick.

Humans work for a purpose. We are designed to create things. I think that being useful is what life is all about.

In the end, living a meaningful life that meets all of your human wants comes from making oneself helpful. Because of this, we get restless when we sleep too much. Too much of a good thing turns into a bad thing, my mother used to say. When I wanted to spend all of my time hanging out with my friends and when I had my first girlfriend, she told me that.

It is real. Like with job, it's bad to sleep too much. Our thoughts and bodies were designed for use. Therefore, the final lesson I took away from doing nothing is that work comes after rest. What happens after work, then? You missed the point if your response was "more work." Probably some sleep is in order.

Time Blocking: Improve Your Focus And Get More Meaningful Work Done

Have you made a list of your priorities or objectives for this year? Do you find it difficult to make time for them? I'm not an exception. Life can be complicated. Most of us multitask a number of different tasks at once. Even while quitting juggling is the obvious solution, it's not always practical. or perhaps essential.

Imagine if you could accomplish more things without wasting time. It is doable. However, you must systematise your labour. Enter: Time blocking is a popular and easy productivity technique. It's neither fancy nor ground-breaking. The only thing you require is a calendar, which can be found on every computer and smartphone.

Utilizing your calendar to schedule time for your top objectives is known as time blocking. You only work on that one thing at that time. And you follow the directions on your schedule. In this manner, you won't have to consider what to do next. But Time Blocking is more than just a technique for increasing productivity. The topic is self-awareness.

The road to high productivity starts with awareness

For instance, writing a book on pragmatic thinking is one of my top priorities for this year. The issue is that I haven't been writing.

How did I arrive at this judgement? I quickly glanced at my list of essentials for 2017, followed by my schedule.

I hadn't set aside any time recently for writing. Do you really need to check your calendar to discover that, you might be asking.

True, I do. I'm not a supercomputer that can recall anything. I'm a typical person. I come up with a plan, get started on it, let life get in the way, and then I FORGET about it.

To everyone of us, it occurs. We require self-awareness and control mechanisms. That is why I enjoy using Time Blocking.

Some people adore time blocking, while others detest it.

Cal Newport, a professor of computer science and the author of Deep Work, also employs time blocking. I take time blocking seriously, spending ten to twenty minutes every evening creating my agenda for the following day, the man claims. I refer to my task lists, calendars, weekly, and quarterly planning notes as I go through this planning process. My objective is to ensure that the appropriate things are advanced at the appropriate rate in order to meet the pertinent dates.

The last line is the main justification for my extensive schedule. Making progress is not the same as working. Additionally, Time Blocking supports me in sharpening my attention so I can complete tasks that matter. Things that actually affect how I live.

I am aware that many prosperous people use blank calendars when working. The articles were read by me. Simply put, they put in two, three, or four hours a day. To be completely honest, I find that to be very alluring as well. One must, however, consider their own personal position. What do you hope to accomplish? And perhaps more importantly: What assets do you possess? People with limited resources frequently have plenty of free time. So why not put it to good use? In either case, I believe that planning has value.

I schedule my days and weeks in advance to ensure that I'm working on the proper things. Too frequently, I become bogged down in finishing daily activities. Consider it in this manner. I'm already quite well organised. And I focus exclusively on one major project in each aspect of my life. But my life spans a wide range of activities, including my family business, blog, podcast, online courses, friendships, and investments.

I may appear to be involved in a variety of activities. However, it depends on how you frame it. One thing drives all I do: having a purposeful, autonomous existence.

But let's not get too lofty at this point. Give time blocking a try if you want to work more efficiently, lack focus, and aren't making any progress. Here are some insights I've gained that might be useful:

• Every night, set aside 10 minutes to organise your day. If you need to make time for other vital tasks, rearrange your blocks.

> For routine chores, use recurring blocks. For instance, I set aside two hours every Tuesday and Thursday to write my newest book.

• Avoid overscheduling. Realistically, you cannot work continuously for ten hours. • Schedule more time than you think you'll need, and give yourself some time in between activities.

Wow, that seems like an excessive amount of planning to me.

No issue. Plan less. For everything, there is always a countermovement. people who promote a lifestyle that is anti-productivity and the complete opposite. People who claim to have empty calendars are generally uninterested in life.

Those who portray themselves as constantly "enjoying" themselves. They enjoy daydreaming and going with the flow. You know what makes me think of that? Ah dude, I didn't have time to study for this subject, the students in school who constantly claimed, but who consistently received straight As. People merely want you to think that they aren't working hard. It's just an act. And when they succeed in life, it appears that it was simple for them. As far as I'm aware, meaningful accomplishments are challenging. Pretending it's simple is not, in my opinion, cool. I also don't think working yourself to death is cool.

Do you consider yourself to be an amateur or a professional?

It is the well-known allegory for finishing work that Steven Pressfield uses in his book The War of Art. The amateur only produces when they are inspired. Every day, the professional sits down and works steadily. Consistent is the key. neither unusual nor excessive.

I Stopped Working Out Daily. Here's What Happened.

I've been giving my life a yearly focus for the past three years. I wanted to work and travel as much as I could in 2014. I set a goal for myself in 2015 to read over 100 books in one year. And I wanted to exercise every day in 2016 as well.

Those are things I've done. Setting a yearlong focus is one of my favourite things to do since it helps you decide what you want to do with your time. If you set your mind to it, you'll be astonished at what you can do in a year. Although it's not going well, I'm still trying, my goal for this year is to write more novels. But I also don't want to quit exercising and reading at the same time.

That's sometimes trickier than it seems, though. I contracted the flu in January of this year. And when I returned to our family business, I didn't realise how much work I still had to do to catch up. For my blog and online classes, I also wanted to keep producing fresh content. I decided to reduce my daily exercise because I couldn't possibly do everything.

BIG MISTAKE

This is what transpired.

- I visited the gym 1-2 times a week rather than exercising every day. I also ran once every week. By the end of January, nothing seemed out of the ordinary, and I was in good health. I also worked hard.

- However, that changed by the end of February. By the end of the day, I was exhausted. an occurrence I never experience

- I also began to write less. I posted two articles a week because I had a large backlog of content.

- I had hit a production ceiling by March. Thankfully, I never stray from my productive routine. I was able to complete the absolute bare minimum of labour. But I gave up making.

In the evening, I started watching Netflix. Even an episode of the TV programme 12 Monkeys caught my attention. It was total crap. Before going to bed, I greatly prefer to read a book.

I became angry at myself for wasting my time.

- In addition, I begin to reflect and journal more when I'm angry.

- I examined my routines. I also saw that I felt exhausted and completed less work.

- Why? Exercise—or more specifically, a lack of it—was the answer.

- By April, I had again changed my focus to getting back in shape.

I'm currently doing it. Additionally, it's critical to know your goals if you want to lose weight and get in shape. For instance, I weigh 181 pounds and am 6'3". However, that is meaningless. The BMI and other widely used metrics are largely meaningless because they reveal nothing about your strength. I don't really care about measurements or even my precise fat percentage, to be honest. Instead, I consider how my fitness affects my daily life. • Run 10K without taking a break when I'm in good form.

- I'll bench press, squat, and deadlift my body weight at least eight times.

- Perform 12 or more pull-ups.

On what is that based? My body and my knowledge. There is no basic guideline in fitness. You must identify your own objective. I believe that a person should be able to lift or push anything that is at least equal to their body weight. You are then better able to carry out your everyday activities. You'll have more energy and attention when you're in terrific physical form.

Want to find your fitness goal?

Create a regimen that's for you—not a 21-year-old bodybuilder—after reading fitness and health-related literature, watching YouTube videos, and speaking with specialists. You are not required to lift weights. Find a physical challenge that you like at the same time. The harsh truth is that your strength and stamina deplete if you don't use them. However, that doesn't imply that you should ignore it. This comparison is similar to one that Zig Ziglar once used to emphasise the significance of motivation: "People frequently remark that motivation doesn't persist. Well, bathing doesn't either, which is why we advise doing it every day.

Therefore, if you don't exercise every day, you aren't helping yourself. Life becomes less enjoyable when you quit exercising. Also, give up trying for quick fixes to feel better. I am aware that most people don't like to hear this counsel. Exercise is difficult. However, that is the whole idea! Your body is the most straightforward tool at your disposal for leading a successful life. Are you fostering it or ignoring it?

If You Want To Be More Productive, Research Shows You Need A Break

Do you work at your desk the most of the time? Do you also have trouble focusing throughout the day? There is an easy way to increase your focus and productivity. "How can I accomplish more while staying focused?"

I get that query rather frequently. Human nature dictates that we constantly seek to produce more. It's simple for machines: you increase speed. Every day, machines improve and become faster. What about your own level of productivity, though? I've read a lot of productivity-related books. I've read a tonne of time-management articles. And I've experimented with several productivity-boosting strategies.

The concept is straightforward: I want to accomplish more in the same amount of time. I have to do less work because I'm not seeking for any tricks or short cuts. Working is fine with me. I dislike feeling like I'm spending time on pointless activities. Sometimes after watching only one YouTube video, I realise that I have been watching for two hours.

I then become angry with YouTube. That, however, is absurd. It's similar to getting irritated with booze after a night of drinking. Alcohol isn't the problem; YOU ARE. You simply couldn't watch one video or take one drink. Could you not? I've discovered a strategy to stop getting frustrated with work-related distractions (not drinking), which makes working much more enjoyable and less stressful.

The answer is easy: After every 30 minutes of work, take a 5-minute rest.

It is often referred to as the Pomodoro method. It's also straightforward why this approach works: biological evolution The human brain is not capable of sustained concentration on a single task. The purpose of our brains is to ensure our survival. The brain is always on alert to shield us from impending hazards. Your brain has a hard time focusing on one item for a prolonged period of time.

Alejandro Lleras' research from the University of Illinois demonstrated that switching between deactivated and activated states at work helps us maintain concentrate. It is best to take brief, scheduled breaks when working on lengthy tasks, such as studying for examinations, giving presentations, or producing reports.

Taking pauses will improve the calibre of your job as well.

By stopping, you force yourself to pause for a moment and reflect. You may occasionally discover that you need to modify your work to improve its quality. In contrast, it's simple to lose focus and become engrossed in your work when you work on a task without taking a break. Because of this, the five-minute breaks are just as crucial as the thirty minutes of labour. Consider your breaks a reward and take them seriously.

Take advantage of your break by going for a short walk, stretching, getting a cup of coffee, or doing something relaxing. Feel good about the effort you did. I've been working for more than a year in 30-minute chunks. I've never completed so much work. Additionally, I enjoy my job more and find it less stressful.

I've tried a variety of breaks and time intervals (25, 30, and 40 minutes), and 45 minutes is about the maximum. Longer durations of concentrate are not beneficial, according to several studies. So that you can test out how long you like to work before taking a break.

Here are a few other items that may be helpful if you decide to try this method:

- To set the 30-minute interval, use an app. I employ Tomighty.
- Only give each 30-minute period one task.
- Don't forget to take breaks.
- Avoid checking your email when on break.
- After every four intervals, take a 15-minute break.
- When you're in a 30-minute period, refuse distractions or phoney crises.

Set a daily objective. For instance, 300 minutes of useful labour are produced by scheduling 10 x 30-minute blocks of time.

With all the commotion, it's simple to overlook the value of taking breaks. You don't need to read any more productivity-related articles. Take a break instead. We occasionally get sidetracked by lists and productivity tricks. The reality is that you still need to put in the effort regardless of what you do to increase your productivity. Therefore, take advantage of the 5-minute pauses to rest.

Part III

Achieving More

Don't Know What You Want? Improve These 7 Universal Skills

What does achievement entail? What are your goals in life? Which profession do you want? The majority of us reply, "I don't know." And what about that? There is nothing improper about that. And yet, we believe that not knowing what you want to do with your life is the worst thing that could ever happen. We exclaim, "OMG! I have no idea what I want!" We then get a severe panic attack. It happens to everyone, so be honest. especially after learning that an old college mate had got hitched. Or perhaps your coworker, who began at the same time as you, recently received a promotion.

We expose our own lack of confidence in life when we are at our most vulnerable. One of the worst mistakes I've ever made was believing I needed to be certain of my particular life goals. In actuality, nobody is aware of their true desires.

Accept The Uncertainty

Tomorrow a cow could mutilate you to death (really happened). On the stock market, you could lose half of your investment. Your property might catch fire. You don't need to know all those things, so I won't. But we must acknowledge that the majority of life's questions remain unanswered. Will you remain wholesome? The stock market could crash. Will your company keep making money? NO ONE IS SURE! That is life's beauty. "If life were predictable, it would cease to be life, and be without flavour," stated Eleanor Roosevelt.

Why do you read so many books, some people ponder. You can't possibly put all you learn to use. They are accurate. I'm unable. Why do I still read about so many varying subjects? I could require a specific piece of knowledge at some point in my life. And should I ever need it, it might completely alter the course of my life. I'll use an illustration. I seriously considered doing it in 2015 after hearing from my friends and mentors that I should impart my productivity, life, and business insights to others.

However, there are other ways to impart your expertise to others. Group training sessions and seminars are both options. Individual coaching is a possibility. You may produce YouTube videos. At conferences, you can present. There are countless options. However, I understood that I should start with written ideas because I've always had a passion for writing and had read so much about it in the past. For me, that was the simplest way to get started.

I had previously studied website development in great detail. Therefore, getting started with all of this was pretty simple for me. In actuality, I made a website in a single day. I then began to write every day for a month. The outcome? A book as well as numerous articles.

Know Where You're Going. Not Your Final Stop.

Years ago, when I studied articles about writing and creating websites, I had no idea that I would later apply those skills to create my own blog. I'll be honest; I had no idea what I desired. All I knew was which way I wanted to travel. I was aware of my desire to contribute and engage in fulfilling job.

Therefore, having a clear idea of what you want to do with your life is not necessary. People evolve. A changing economy. Therefore, making the bold claim "I know what I want!" is not really conceivable. All people really require is a sense of direction. a picture of your ideal future.

You don't have to be certain of your destination, believe me. People who claim to always know what they want are frequently mentioned in the media. But only a small number of people fall into that category. Personally, I've never encountered somebody like that. Most of us don't start off with that conviction. It develops with time.

If you're stuck trying to figure out where you want to go in life, that's automatically your top priority in life. In one of my all-time favourite business books, Getting Everything You Can Out of All You've Got, Jay Abraham makes a similar recommendation: "Your first priority is to determine what you want. Then, make sure you pursue the path that will lead to that." Nothing is more heartbreaking than witnessing a person reach the age of 75 or 80 and look back unhappily due to having pursued the incorrect aim.

You see that he doesn't suggest that you should be certain of your goals? That is not practical at all. Instead, we must be aware of our general direction. I am aware that it is still elusive. But that's the only practical response I've ever across in my life.

Work On Universal Skills

Don't squander your time binge-watching TV, drinking alcohol, or indulging in junk food while you're working everything out. Use your time wisely. Pick up skills that you can always use. Want some motivation? Here are several abilities I'm always trying to improve:

1. Self-Control: Practice ignoring the critical voice in your thoughts. Leave your bed now. Visit the gym. Never pay attention to "I don't want to."

2. Personal Effectiveness: Discover how to get the most out of the 16 to 18 hours you are awake. Do more things more effectively.

3. Communication: We all believe that we are skilled communicators. But the fact is, we're terrible. Communication is a science and an art. And it's essential to our capacity for collaboration.

4. You always engage in negotiations. with your partner, partner's children, children's parents, teachers, friends, coworkers, managers, etc. Learn to negotiate deals that benefit all sides.

5. Persuasion: Discover ethical ways to achieve what you desire.

Physical stamina and strength are other important factors. Make your own progress. Every person should be capable of doing it.

7. Flexibility: Sitting all day at your desk or in a car makes you a stiff person. The most typical weak regions of desk workers, your hips, lower back, hamstrings, and calves, can all benefit from stretching.

If you want to do it well, there is enough there to keep you busy for a lifetime. Choose a skill that makes you happy. Make progress in it. then select a different. Continue doing that process over and over. You'll understand what you desire soon enough. And even if you don't, nothing terrible will happen. There is still much to discover.

Leave The Office On Time and Don't Take Your Work Home

Every person who wishes to have a successful, lengthy, and fulfilling career should learn these two lessons. However, following that instruction is quite challenging. I didn't realise it for the first six years of my profession. Furthermore, I still have to remind myself that life is more important than my job.

In the majority of the places I've worked before, there was a "perception is reality" culture. That implies that appearances matter more than truth. In other words, it seems that the employee who has been there the longest is also the hardest worker. That might be the case now.

But it is not important. Results are the only thing that matter, as we all know. But as a group, we insist on focusing on vanity variables like attendance at meetings, number of hours worked, and email response time. It's pitiful. We encourage everyone at our family business to depart when their shift is over. We've discovered that focusing on priorities is a far better metric than just taking a person's employment hours into consideration.

And yet, saying "I've fulfilled my top priority, I'm going home" still causes people discomfort. I got it. You don't want to make your coworkers feel awful or treated unfairly when you're working in a group. But consider the reason you started working in the first place. To contribute, you are there. to the business you work for or your own.

Working Too Long Is Unproductive

I'm sure people enjoy spending ten hours a day in your company, but it doesn't mean you have to remain there for as long as it makes you unproductive. Because this is a major factor in why we no longer work conventional 9 or 10 hour days. It's not useful.

Numerous studies have demonstrated that working long hours is ineffective. Working too much and the stress that comes with it can cause heart disease, memory loss, insomnia, and depression. You see what I mean. Because of this, my first work rule is:

Leave promptly

I recently mentioned to my mentor how wonderful it is to love your profession. I've never worked a job I didn't love, he declared. It's one of life's most satisfying experiences. However, "too much of a good thing turns bad," as my mother likes to say. I think the same applies to job. I'm not referring to intensity here.

Don't get me wrong; I put in a lot of effort. Have done for ever. Just be careful not to ramble on. Knowing when to stop working hard is a skill. But that's really difficult, as my mentor said to me: "My biggest difficulty was that I worked too much. At 7 AM, I left the house, and I returned at 11 PM. That's excessive.

You must take precautions to avoid taking on too much work. It is simple as well. Simply get out of the office on time. It doesn't matter if you enjoy your job or not. Go home when it's time to!

You are not required to work around the clock. Your ego alone can. In all honesty, the office will be open on Monday. They will still be alive, your coworkers. Your business won't fail.

The goal of work is to produce results. If you are ineffective if you can't accomplish that in 6 to 8 hours per day. Therefore, read a book on personal effectiveness or enrol in productivity training instead of working overtime.

Leave Your Work At Work

Don't simply leave for home and bring your work, though. That negates the entire goal. Nobody finds it cool to close transactions over the phone while having supper. Additionally, thinking about work constantly when at home is not beneficial to you.

Rest a little. Take a Call of Duty game. Prepare a meal for your partner. Take a stroll with the kids. Whatever. You see, leading a happy life is really rather easy. Everything is under our control. We are free to choose what brings us joy. "Very little is needed to build a happy existence; it is all inside yourself, in your way of thinking," said Marcus Aurelius, and I have printed it on my journal to serve as a reminder of this.

Money, wealth, popularity, or recognition do not, in and of themselves, bring us happiness, as we all know. Nevertheless, we put in excessive effort to get things that don't really make us happy in the first place.

Why then do we continue to work so much that it harms us? Perhaps it's our ego. Perhaps we're powerless to stop ourselves. It varies depending on the individual. I don't really care what the cause is. I just know that working too much lowers the quality of both your life and your work.

What counts is that we safeguard ourselves against our own foolishness. We resemble children. To live happily and safely, we need rules. We must leave the office on time as a result, which is the first rule of work. We don't bring our work home is the second rule. The third rule, then? Let's put that off for the time being. We'll discuss that afterwards. I should head home now.

Consistency Is Key: Improve By 0.1% Every Day

Do you ever stress over things beyond your control? If so, welcome to the club. To everyone of us, it occurs. However, worrying is a time and energy waster. Think about the following scenario: You offend a client by making a mistake at work. Perhaps you emailed the wrong person. You might overlook a problem to tackle. It makes no difference what it is. Imagine a severe mishap occurring at work.

When you learn, what do you do? Do you worry a lot? You feel uneasy? You are to blame? Accuse others? Do you believe your career is over? We fixate on things we can't control when things go wrong, which makes us our own worst enemies.

Reading about these topics is one thing. Implementing it in real life is a very different matter. Because panicking when sh*t hits the fan is only normal. Instead of pondering, stand back and concentrate on the things you can manage. What are you in charge of? In essence, we are solely in control of our own thoughts and behaviours.

We determine our:

- Desire
- Attitude
- Judgments
- Determination

I think that's it. We have no control over anything else. Therefore, worrying about items that are not on that list is pointless.

That is a practise in Stoic philosophy. anything that has been around for ages. The best part is that you can start using this in your life right away. Focus on the things you can control the next time you find yourself fretting about a scenario. Since there is nothing else we can do, what matters is that we act morally. We have no influence over results. You see?

1. Made an error? Adjust it.

2. A problem occurs? Make a decision.

Don't be shocked when awful things occur either. Instead, prepare for them to occur. You won't ever be taken off guard if you do it that way.

Similarly, avoid whining and asking "why me!" when you experience terrible luck. Accept it instead, and then put all of your effort towards coming up with a solution. Always have a positive outlook.

Why doing this activity makes you more productive.

What does philosophy have to do with productivity is a question I get asked a lot. The most crucial factor in productivity, then, is consistency.

It's not about having epiphanies, getting your big break, staying up all night, or consuming Red Bull all day to be productive. It's important to strive for daily improvement if you want to accomplish something in your life. Every day, you want to work out, read, work, learn, and study.

Results suffer when there is inconsistency.

To increase my mental toughness, I adhere to the philosophies of the Stoics and Pragmatists. It plays a significant role in Procrastinate Zero, my personal productivity strategy.

Ups and downs are undesirable to me since they reduce productivity. Instead, I'd like to make 0.1 percent more progress each day of the year. And that's a really doable objective. Try it; it might just transform your life as well.

Who Says You Have To Get Out Of Your Comfort Zone?

I cherish my comfort zone. That, in my opinion, is where the real magic happens. My family, friends, coworkers, my job, music, literature, movies, my bike, the gym, the park—you name it—are all in my comfort zone. whatever I adore. I'm more willing to take risks and attempt new things when I'm in that safe space. The concept behind that silly little image has never made sense to me. You understand what I'm referring to, right?

"Your comfort level." a little circle

Where the magic takes place. A large circle representing the prospect of achievement.

It's absurd to think that "magic" can only occur when you venture outside of your comfort zone. While we're at it, why act like your comfort zone is a terrible thing? This pitiful small circle is contrasted with the larger "magical" circle.

Yes, I completely support pushing oneself, trying new things, progressing, developing, etc. But unlike many well-known self-help experts, I don't think being in your comfort zone is a terrible thing.

You may call me cynical. Count me as stoic. But I'm just a realistic person first and foremost. Additionally, you shouldn't really step too far outside of your comfort zone. In truth, I think that "magic" comes slowly.

The 'Magic' that people talk about is where?

I've discovered that when I'm not stressed about money, making new friends, adjusting to a foreign environment, or anything else associated with constantly travelling around, I work at my best.

Don't get me wrong, though. I won't say that I like to stay put. For me, stagnation is a death sentence. There are, in my opinion, various stages of life. You invest in yourself when you take it slowly, concentrate on your abilities and character. Additionally, there are instances when you simply have to take a chance. It's not worth living a wimpy life.

However, those two things are linked. You won't ever take a chance if you don't improve yourself and if you lack confidence. I've wanted to do what I'm doing now for years. But rather than stepping outside of my comfort zone (which was terrifying), I gradually took on new and more difficult projects.

I first earned two business degrees. Then my father and I launched a business. It happened in 2010. And after two years of spending six or seven days a week on that business, I began doing freelance marketing work. Again, I got a position at a research advisory firm because I wanted to experience working for a large organisation after a few years of freelancing and launching (and failing) other enterprises on my own.

And after doing that for a year and a half, I made the decision to start blogging and talking about entrepreneurship, career, and productivity online. I had been engaging in the activities I write about by that time for more than ten years. I merely share what I've learned; I don't have all the answers.

Therefore, it would be absurd for me to join those who shout, "All it takes to succeed is to venture outside your comfort zone." NOW!" Have you ever pushed yourself past your comfort zone? It doesn't matter how little, either. So what did you discover? A leprechaun carrying cash, perhaps?

Not going to happen.

That storey about the comfort zone is nonsense. You don't have to believe it if you don't want to; it just might inspire some folks. It's similar to when individuals assert that you must get up early if you want to succeed. claims who? I firmly believe that stepping outside of your comfort zone will only result in more work for you. It's not at all fancy. There is no use of magic. Nothing except tears, sweat, and blood.

Work Your Way Up from a Comfortable Position

I believe that the majority of readers of this kind of content have goals in mind. You might wish to leave your work, launch a business, expand an existing one, start an art career, write a book, or whatever.

You presumably likely realise that it's difficult. Why then do you act in a way that makes you feel extremely uncomfortable and makes things worse for yourself? Instead, begin at the bottom. Lay a solid foundation. Get comfy before doing anything scary.

"What's the appearance of that foundation?"

If you want to live stress-free, you should have enough money in your savings account to cover your expenses for six months in case something bad happens. Think of it as a backup plan. That's my pragmatic thinking speaking once more. Do some math to determine what that number is for you. And before you have that money in your savings account, don't even consider taking a chance.

Develop a skill set that is valuable as well. I don't care about money because I have faith in my capacity to get employment, which is one of the reasons. I'll find a method to get job the following day even if I go bankrupt tomorrow. In my schooling, I've put years of work and hundreds of thousands of dollars. How would you describe your skill? What value can you add to the world? What issues can you fix? Other components of your foundation include:

One. Family. Make a family if you don't already have one.

2. Companions Not everyone can be your friend. The few individuals you stick to will also stick to you.

three. You. Improve your body and mind consciously. Every night, go to bed a little stronger and wiser.

Finally, avoid attempting to be someone you're not. Do not pretend that you can work in a boiler room if you are an introvert. Don't pretend you can work alone if you're an extrovert. Avoid pushing yourself so hard that your life becomes miserable; instead, stay close to yourself.

In the end, we all require comfort since it is a fundamental human need. Growth is necessary, though. Don't, under any circumstances, spend too much time in your comfort zone. Make an effort to advance daily: Regardless of how small the step is. No magic. only an effort

If You Can Believe It, You Can Achieve It

I am aware of your thoughts. This person is claiming that nothing is impossible after likely reading a motivating quote on social media. Oh, okay. I don't believe there is a dearth of inspirational articles, books, films, or Facebook posts in the globe. A larger dose of Monday motivation is not necessary. Do you understand the reason? It's not practical to have that kind of motivation. It makes no difference. It is useless. Similar to consuming Red Bull, It swiftly vanishes.

On the other hand, belief is a very effective instrument. And many people underuse it. The issue is that the majority of us don't believe. And when I discuss believing, I do so from a standpoint of application. I'm not referring to optimism or religion. You can't just "hope" for the best and wait for wonderful things to happen to you, in my opinion. Hope is not a viable life strategy. Want a pragmatic, I like to look at the facts and draw conclusions. Whether you like it or not, everything that is floating about in your thoughts is there because you think it to be true.

"Life stinks,"

- "I don't do my job well."
- "I never manage to land my ideal job."

No one adores me,

- "I'll never be prosperous."

See? You believe those things, so it's all there. The easiest way to describe it is by quoting William James, one of the key personalities linked with pragmatism: "Belief will help generate the fact."

You can use belief as a useful tool to sculpt reality.

Have you ever thought of choosing your own beliefs? not your family, friends, coworkers, or even the media. You make a decision based on your observations of the world. Because of this, belief produces facts. No, an R. Kelly song is not how life is. No matter how much you want to believe it, you cannot fly. A realist always keeps things as they are.

Without putting forth the effort, you will never develop into a respectable leader. Unless you take action, nothing will ever change in your life.

However, that is not the issue. As you are aware. Without taking action, nothing happens.

All that matters is whether you think you can or can't lead the life you want. That's all there is to it. However, you have to genuinely believe it. Saying you believe something is one thing. To genuinely believe that is something very different. Let me illustrate that with a personal storey. The majority of my life, I experienced fear. It all began in school. People warned me: "If you don't earn high grades, you won't get into a good institution. Without a decent degree, you won't ever find a job.

My seventeen-year-old brain entered full-fledged terror mode after hearing it. I began to believe that ridiculous tale.

Who desires to live as a pauper and pass away alone?

That is a metaphor for having no confidence in oneself. Since it always seems to be the alternative. It's a frequent misconception that if you take a chance or do something unusual, you'll end yourself homeless. Many of the people I meet claim to have made crucial life decisions out of fear.

- Do you detest your position yet hesitate to change it for fear of losing your home?

- Do you wish to leave your partner but are worried that you'll pass away alone yourself?

• Are you studying yourself to death out of concern for what your parents will say if you drop out?

• Do you withhold your work from the public out of fear that someone may pelt you with objects because you're a failure?

Will that actually occur? Or are you just having a mental meltdown? Most likely the latter. I've always wished I could write. I used to compose poems for my sweetheart in high school. It was quite pitiful, but hey, she liked my strange poems. However, joking aside, I really enjoyed reading and writing down my ideas.

But instead, every adult I encountered was out to kill me. "Writing is not a viable career." They very likely had it right. It's challenging to support oneself as a writer.

Then what? Everything worthwhile is challenging. At the time, I was unaware of that. I therefore abandoned my objective. I made the wise choice to go the safe route and get a business degree. I don't regret making that choice because I've gained a lot of knowledge. However, the entire ordeal made me a terrified being. Because of the terrifying experience in school, I eventually lost faith in myself. I put my writing and reading on hold. And it's a complete waste of time that I could have spent honing my abilities.

You are capable of anything (as long as you believe in it).

What did you formerly believe but have since abandoned out of fear? We've probably all been there. You're going to stay there forever if you don't take care.

For me, it wasn't until two or three years ago that I realised that you can use believe as a tool to help you reach your objectives. I somehow stumbled upon pragmatism in my reading (which is a way of thinking). And it entirely altered the way I think. I came to see the futility of having no self-confidence. I made the decision to start thinking that I could have the life I wanted.

Of course, I'm not yet fully covering my expenses with my writing. I work as a consultant and own a business. But my blog does bring in some revenue. And for the seventeen-year-old version of me, that's really useful information to know. It is quite easy to believe in yourself. You too can succeed. Just keep in mind that belief is a tool. That notion is not at all novel. It has existed for many centuries. Just different names used by different people.

Whatever name you choose, I don't care. But given that I've been employing believe as a tool, guess what happened? Now, most of what I formerly believed is true. And the other things that I think will one day be proven to be true.

How do I know for sure? because that is conceivable in my opinion. You can accomplish anything your mind can imagine. That is not a quote meant to inspire. That is true. Do you think so?

Don’t Compete. Create!

You are as mistaken as I was if you believe that you must compete for better jobs or a larger market share. We have a deep-seated belief in competition. We think that other people and ourselves must compete for the same occupations. If someone has a job, it follows that you cannot hold that same position. Additionally, you must compete with that company to "gain" a portion of their market share if they have a specific market share.

At least, that is the counsel that is generally accepted. Additionally, it's what I studied in business school. The foundation of my entire schooling was commercial competition. Additionally, practically every business book I've read makes the assumption that there is competition in business.

They are completely mistaken. You are practising restricted thinking when you believe that you must compete with other companies or people for resources like money, employment, or attention. Instead, we must embrace an attitude of abundance. You get rid of the concept of competition, as one of the first well-known personal development authors Wallace D. Wattles put it. You should be creating, not vying for previously produced works. There is nothing you need to take from anyone.

The primary error of typical business thinking is their assumption that there is a finite amount of supply. However, it isn't always the case. But even if that were the case, having that attitude is detrimental. I believe that the majority of individuals, both business owners and employees, worry that someone else will "beat them to it."

Right? We worry that if we lose our customers, business, contracts, or attention, we will also lose everything else we have fought so hard to obtain. But the issue is just that. Fear feeds on itself. What will happen if you're worried that you won't be able to grow? Yes, you won't develop!

History reveals that humankind has consistently advanced. Yes, there have been periods of war and economic hardship, but we have always bounced back and expanded. Therefore, if you predict that the global economy won't expand, you're basically betting against humanity! That is not what I think. Humans constantly manage to thrive and survive. Simply put, it is what we do.

You have to think that there is plenty in the world. For everyone, there are adequate opportunities and resources. Therefore, never let yourself believe that you won't succeed. What's the use of that?

If You Can't Find The Right Career, Create One

Life isn't always easy, you know. Finding a job that truly fulfils you on a mental and financial level is also difficult. I am aware that this problem affects a lot of people. I am aware that many of these individuals place limitations on themselves by believing they are unable to build a profession.

I believe that individuals should establish careers in a manner similar to how I think businesses and entrepreneurs should create market share. It was unusual for me to meet a "Chief Happiness Officer" at a non-tech company. I looked into it, and it seems that in 2003, Ronald McDonald was the first person to hold the CHO title. After that, tech firms began using the name. It is extremely easy. The health and happiness of workers is under the purview of the CHO. I also learned that Tony Hsieh, the CEO of Zappos, is a strong proponent of worker satisfaction.

But here's the thing: Traditional businesses believe it to be nonsense. The business I described earlier initially agreed with that notion. Of course, they lacked a CHO position. She informed me that the post needed to be created. Leaders once held the view that compensation is the only factor influencing a person's decision to work for you. The people you attract improve as you give more money.

For some, that might be accurate. Money, however, is not necessarily a good thing. Many people place more importance on enjoying oneself at work, feeling valued, and being content. And the CHO is successful at doing that.

It doesn't matter what other people think, that's the thing. Go for it if you can provide value to it and you believe in it. People will always say things like, "No one needs this," "Your work is crap," and "You're wasting your time."

Don't pay attention to the doubters. Let them become lost in their own constricting ideas. Do this instead:

Produce, Produce, Produce.

Everybody has access to enough opportunities in the world. The issue is that the majority of individuals miss out on the opportunity. Go out there and build your career if that's what you want to do. The same is valid for your company. And don't pay attention to obstacles like a lack of funding, doubters, or other reasons why you shouldn't. Adopt a mindset of abundance. You'll soon have so many opportunities that you won't know what to do with them.

That is referred to as a "luxury problem" in The Netherlands. It's the only issue you want to have, I assure you.

All Strength Comes From Repetition

Ignoring the fundamentals of your profession is the biggest error you can make. No matter what you do, where you live, or who you are, this is true.

You can never be consistent if you ignore the principles that make you a good person, athlete, friend, businessperson, student, etc. The most important lesson I took away from observing athletes was that. Professional athletes under constant pressure to perform well.

Consider former Olympic wrestler and current UFC Light Heavyweight Champion Daniel Cormier. The champion's 38-year-old career thus far has been spectacular. As a wrestler, he gained numerous gold medals. Additionally, he has triumphed in 20 out of his 22 MMA contests. He is regarded as among the best.

Additionally, he co-hosts UFC Tonight on Fox Sports and works as a combat sports analyst. The man is really energetic. What, in his own opinion, is the secret to his success? sticking to the fundamentals You can't reach the greatest levels of the sport without having the fundamentals in place, he asserts.

That applies to all aspects of life; it's not only true for sports. You name it: speaking, selling, writing, or leading. You won't ever reach your maximum potential if the fundamentals aren't in order.

Repeat The Basics

And repetition is the only way to get better at the fundamentals. By repeatedly lifting weights, you become stronger. Anaerobic exercise helps you gain stamina. That is common knowledge. How about your thoughts, though? How may one develop mental strength? What purpose does it even serve? The solution is easy: The mind is where everything begins. The War of Art author Steven Pressfield summed it up best: "Long-term, we must start to establish our inherent capabilities. Not only do you need computer technology abilities. It's the traditional fundamentals of independence, motivation, reinforcement, self-discipline, and self-command.

But I was continuously asking, "How do you do that?" I know how to build up my physical strength. But I've never known how to strengthen my mind. And I always believed there had to be a better way whenever someone said to me, "It's all about life experience." Who wants to become intellectually strong at the age of 70, let's face it?

Some tasks can be completed more quickly, especially if you continually going over the fundamentals. Because we make mistakes the majority of the time then. We believe that we are experts.

Stay A Beginner

How frequently do you tell yourself, "I know that"? Quite often, if you're like the majority of us. We must constantly remind ourselves that the biggest losers in life are the ones who believe they are infallible. I frequently encounter individuals who believe they are all-knowing. I also don't even mention online users. A lot of commentators like to demonstrate their intelligence by saying things like these are "so clear." Well, the wisest individuals in the world don't think that way. "It's the repetition of affirmations that leads to belief," once stated Muhammad Ali. Things start to happen after that conviction solidifies into a belief.

You won't just become great if you keep doing the fundamentals; you will also stay great. It's a problem that all top achievers deal with. In many aspects of my life, including fitness, philosophy, kindness, business, and writing, I repeat the fundamentals. For instance, I mentally exercise by rereading my favourite texts on stoicism each month. I frequently go to Strunk & White's The Elements Of Style to review the fundamentals of clear and concise writing.

If I don't keep repeating these ideas, I'll forget my life philosophy and how to write quality articles. That is how the brain functions. Without repetition, we are prone to forgetting things. I've always thought of myself as a novice. One of the first—and most crucial—lessons I picked up from my mentor was that. Even though he is now in his 70s, he still sees himself as a student of life.

The same way I conduct business. I continually return to the inquiry, "What is the purpose of a business?" You need to repeat the fundamentals if your response is "to make money," as I can tell you.

It's quite easy: Discover the fundamentals of your field. And say them again. Ensure simplicity. Repeating harmful, incorrect, or negative things is the biggest time waster there is. The only thing you need to be careful of is that. Never follow advise from someone who hasn't done something effectively themselves.

Be Great. Stay Great.

Look, you can be really intelligent, motivated, humble, etc., but what good is it if you don't stay that way? How frequently do you see people achieve success only to waste it? Have you ever witnessed a one-hit wonder?

Exactly. The best ones are the only ones that endure. And you must never undervalue the power of repetition if you want to stay here as well. Never believe that you are successful or intelligent enough. Because you stay excellent with that mentality.

How I Measure My Life

By examining the figures, you can quickly assess a business. Employee churn, turnover, profit, costs, etc. However, how do you assess your life? There are no standardised ways to evaluate your life. Therefore, it is up to each individual to develop a system for determining their current position in life. Some people determine this by comparing their income to that of their peers. Some people consider their corporate career progression. Others evaluate themselves based on their appearance.

I've researched how today's greatest thinkers evaluate their lives. The response is unexpected. Rarely do you read of successful people who base their quality of life on their bank balance or any other conventional metric. Instead, those who are regarded as successful in the eyes of society frequently consider these three things:

1. Power

2. Work

3. Connections

I've tried to make all three of the aforementioned improvements. I've discovered that they are all connected in some way. I work more effectively when I'm in a good mood and have a lot of energy. Additionally, when I produce better work, I feel content with my life and am able to be more generous with the people in it. And that strengthens my connections. And what is the key to living a happy life? favourable connections. How Will You Measure Your Life? author and Harvard Business School professor Clayton M. Christensen asserts that our relationships with our family and close friends are the single most significant contributor to our long-term happiness.

Quality is more important than quantity in relationships. Even if it's simple to criticise those who use social media, I still believe it's important to state that nobody cares how many online friends or followers you have.

Growing genuine relationships takes time. Additionally, they are unconditional. Most partnerships are not sincere. We only truly love someone until, for instance, they alter their opinions or put on a few pounds. Or, we only invite pals to our birthday parties if they accompany us on outings and buy us beer.

Such conditional partnerships have little value. True love and friendship are more powerful than that. You always stand behind the ones you love. That enriches life.

1. Measuring Energy

It's simple to gauge your energy. You only need to consider how you feel physically. I recently written precisely about that. Finding strategies to have more energy is what important. What simple action can I take today that will have a big influence on my energy? is a good place to start. Everyone can agree with the following:

1. Work out every day. I do interval runs twice a week, four times a week of weightlifting, and on days I don't work out, I make sure to walk for at least 30 minutes at a fast pace.

2. Eat healthily; I don't adhere to any one diet. I consume a variety of foods that are considered to be unhealthy, including meat, bread, pasta, and others. But I feel fantastic. I simply avoid processed foods, and I consume very little sugar (I like chocolate). Additionally, I don't take in more calories than I expend.

That's a contributing factor. Every day when I accomplish those two things, I feel wonderful. And I feel quite energetic. I get depressed as soon as I stop exercising or start eating poorly. This is how I know it functions. By increasing your exercise and eating healthy, you can simply increase your energy.

2. Measuring Work

I don't consider money, social standing, or other general metrics when it comes to my job. Instead, I consider how much I still have to learn. To put it another way: Have you utilised all of your learning potential? Why do I consider education but not income? because it's more important. In How Will You Measure Your Life?, Christensen puts it succinctly: "You need to keep looking for situations that you think are worthwhile, in which you will be able to learn new things, to achieve, and in which you will be given more and more responsibility to carry, if you want to truly discover pleasure," said Albert Einstein.

Success in life and career is directly correlated with learning capacity. And perhaps more significantly, how much you continue to learn. Learning never stops. Additionally, your ability to learn is directly correlated with your income. You can increase your income by learning more. It is real. Of course, this assertion has its limitations. Additionally, knowledge must always be applied.

Everyone has heard about intelligent individuals who failed to realise their full potential. You must constantly act on what you know if you want to succeed. Knowledge is useless if it is not put to use. However, in general, the more information you have (via education or experience), the more you can offer your employer, coworkers, clients, etc. Contribution also results in income.

3. Measuring Relationships

What you'll discover is that your relationships will improve as a result of the more you give to the lives of other people. And that last component brings everything full circle. Stick entirely to yourself when evaluating your connections. Do not make the largest error that most people do, which is to focus on what others do for us. You run the risk of starting to keep score if you don't.

Wayne Dyer, who is no longer with us, once remarked, "How people treat you is their karma; how you react is yours." Measure how much time and effort you invest in your relationships rather than how other people treat you. You have complete power just over that. My personal observation is that relationships flourish when you make time for the people that matter to you. If they don't, the relationship probably wasn't meant to be. The only option is to continue. The main takeaway from this is that we should constantly concentrate on the things we can control.

All of these factors are under our direct control, including our energy, effort, and relationship-related efforts. One of the most important truths that philosophers from all cultures and eras impart to us is this. Take stock of your life. Feelings should be quickly evaluated. You just need to make improvements at this point.

Why You Should Live Like You're Immortal

My peers all seem to believe that not having a fulfilling life is okay because one is young. However, millennials are not the only generation to rationalise their behaviour. All of us do. I got it. Life's obligations can be terrifying. Having avocado on toast is much cooler. You know what else is cool, though?

• Establishing a fulfilling career that makes you proud.

• Making a difference in other people's lives.

• Developing a beneficial good or service.

• Putting money into investments for retirement.

Yes, but I'm still young, you say. "Tomorrow is always an option." C'mon. Quit hiding! Why are you holding out? I want to provide one piece of advice to everyone out there who isn't happy: Begin living as though you are eternal.

I am aware that it sounds strange. I'll explain in two minutes. According to conventional wisdom, life is not eternal.

- "Life is short!"
- "YOLO!"
- "Live now!"

And I also concur with that. However, if you live your life in accordance with that concept, nothing that doesn't pay off right away makes sense. Why on earth would you accomplish difficult things if you believe that life is short? It is not logical. According to their viewpoint, it's preferable to spend your money, go out every week, drink a lot, and live lavishly.

What does all of that lead to, you ask?

That query doesn't require a scientific explanation. The response is "nothing" There is yet another way to look at life today: a permanent presence for you.

Consider this. If I informed you that you wouldn't die, how would your life change? I used to live as if I were mortal when I look in the mirror. I would buy clothes, toys, and vacations with my money. I, too, seemed to be rushing, though. I had a long list of goals for my life. And ideally very quickly.

I also pursued numerous goals at once. similar to a dog. pursuing everything that is dazzling. or even following my own illogical notions. But recently, I've changed my perspective. The question "What if I were immortal?" is included. I am aware that it appears as though I am developing a hyperbolic chamber that offers endless life. But be assured, I'm not that naive. I'm using metaphor here. I originally had this thought after reading "Think of yourself as dead" in one of Marcus Aurelius' Meditations. Your life is now over. Take what is left now and live well.

I'm focusing on the final sentence, "Living properly." Why does that matter? Everyone, in my opinion, has a unique perspective. I define living properly as being content with my existence. that I can really say, "I like my life," when I look in the mirror. When I opted to live in the here and now, was I actually happy? Not really, no. I lacked a legitimate employment, a home, or anything else I could be proud of. Why was that, then? I was too preoccupied with the present. I expected things to move quickly.

"You'll be dead before you realise it," he said. That frame of mind is now suitable for beginning. Telling someone they're going to die is the best way to kick them in the butt. But thinking that way when you're trying to construct a LIFE is not helpful. Being present is wonderful, but like with many other things in life, moderation is key.

I like to live as though I'm immortal because of this. Since, if you live forever...

• You have endless time to construct something.

• There isn't a deadline to meet; • You can make mistakes and grow from them.

• You should treat others with respect because they will also exist eternally.

This minor change in perspective has enabled me to adopt a new perspective on life. I don't mind looking out 10 or 20 years. That supports my decision-making TODAY. For instance, I'd rather invest or save my money than spend it because "future Paul" will profit from doing so.

"But Paul, what about now?"

I did mention being satisfied, after all. Oddly enough, I find that saving money makes me happier. Or when I regularly exercise or eat well. This concept's effectiveness fascinates me when I consider it. We're all aware that death is coming (I recently even wrote an article about it). That is both excellent and bad.

• It's advantageous because it creates urgency.

• Negative because we fail to see the big picture.

Which way do you eat? a human being who is mortal or immortal? I hope your life is everything you want it to be. Because ultimately, that's what counts the most.

The Power Of Compounding: You Can Achieve Anything, If You Stop Trying To Do Everything

Do you have a big list of aspirations for the future? Do you wish to find out more? More money? Boost your abilities? maximise the potential of your connections? Better living?

Everything there is beneficial. It's all about advancement and moving forward in life. One crucial aspect of all this labouring, hustle, striving, and achieving more is that you can't do it all at once. That makes perfect sense, right? Time and energy are resources that are limited. As a result, if you take on too much, you become overworked. Instead, concentrating your efforts on a single task will be considerably more successful.

Success Adds Up

We achieve real achievement when we concentrate on one issue at a time. I originally learned about that concept in high school. I made the decision to focus exclusively on one subject at a time while I was studying for my final exams. And after I had a firm understanding of the content, I only moved on to the next.

I discovered that if I engaged myself in something for a few days, I could learn it much more quickly. The majority of my friends studied several courses each day. That strategy never appeals to me since it is too disorganised. I don't take on a major project when I'm working on one at work. I don't begin writing a book while constructing a new course for my blog. That method enables me to do tasks more quickly and effectively. So when I focus on one subject, I do considerably more.

The One Thing, a fantastic book by Gary Keller and Jay Papasan that explores this idea, sums it up best: "When I'd had significant success, I had limited my concentrate to one thing, and where my success varied, my focus had too."

Do you have a lot of projects going on? Are you not focused on a single thing? There is a good probability that you won't get the best outcomes. Or even worse: If you try to accomplish multiple goals at once, you can fail. Simple logic explains why: The majority of us think that success comes all at once. The reality is otherwise. The quote from Keller and Papasan, "Success is sequential, not simultaneous," is excellent.

It all adds up. You pick up a new skill. another follows. You complete one task. another follows. Your successes accumulate over time to become an astounding feat.

Particularly in the case of money. Most people accumulate wealth over time. Most folks don't make a lot of money. Forget about the Evan Spiegels and Conor McGregors of the world. These individuals are career lottery winners. But to achieve in life, you don't need a unique talent or set of talents. You are more likely to lead a fulfilling life if you take the long route, cross each objective off your list one at a time, and gradually increase your money. It's easy. It always works, too. Those who argue that it doesn't just haven't had the time to put it into practise in their own lives.

One of my mentors is the owner of a couple dozen million-dollar residences. Over time, he accumulated his money. He is now in his seventies. Things do, in fact, take time. And the best outcomes are obtained when patience and compounding are combined. And these are not unusual occurrences. I won't guarantee you the next Zuckerberg or a gold medal at the 2020 Olympics. Anyone may increase their abilities, save money, and build wealth.

Thanks For Reading

I appreciate you reading this article all the way through. I respect the fact that you chose to focus your attention on one book rather than any of the countless other things you could have done. Every piece of material I produce has the intention of sharing something I wish someone had told me sooner.

CPSIA information can be obtained
at www.ICGtesting.com
Printed in the USA
LVHW021317031222
734485LV00013B/1010

9 781944 237264